Moragh Carter (whose first name is pronounced Mora) is an English writer who befriended Jack & Misty after hearing their song 'Tennessee Birdwalk' on internet radio in 2004. They first met in April 2007 and their friendship continues to grow. Moragh got tired of waiting for Jack to write their autobiography and decided to write their story herself.

In Harmony

A biography of

Jack Blanchard and Misty Morgan

MORAGH CARTER

Copyright © 2012 Moragh Carter

The moral right of the author has been asserted.

Apart from any fair dealing for the purposes of research or private study, or criticism or review, as permitted under the Copyright, Designs and Patents Act 1988, this publication may only be reproduced, stored or transmitted, in any form or by any means, with the prior permission in writing of the publishers, or in the case of reprographic reproduction in accordance with the terms of licences issued by the Copyright Licensing Agency. Enquiries concerning reproduction outside those terms should be sent to the publishers.

Matador
9 Priory Business Park,
Wistow Road, Kibworth Beauchamp,
Leicestershire. LE8 0RX
Tel: (+44) 116 279 2299
Fax: (+44) 116 279 2277
Email: books@troubador.co.uk
Web: www.troubador.co.uk/matador

ISBN 978 1780884 202

British Library Cataloguing in Publication Data.
A catalogue record for this book is available from the British Library.

Typeset in 11pt Aldine401 BT Roman by Troubador Publishing Ltd, Leicester, UK

Matador is an imprint of Troubador Publishing Ltd

*I dedicate this book to my dear friends, Jack and Misty,
without whose input it could not have been written,
and whose songs have given me,
and their many fans, so much enjoyment.*

Contents

Chapter 1 - Introduction ... 1

Chapter 2 - Jack's Early Life ... 4

Chapter 3 – Misty's Early Life ... 16

Chapter 4 - Starting Out Together ... 20

Chapter 5 - Hitting the Big Time ... 31

Chapter 6 - Down From the Heights ... 53

Chapter 7 - Out of the Limelight ... 59

Chapter 8 - New Beginnings ... 63

Chapter 9 - Jack's Stories - a short selection ... 79

Chapter 10 - Further Insights ... 93

Chapter 11 - The Rewards of Success ... 103

Chapter 12 - The Last Word ... from Jack ... 120

Acknowledgements ... 122

The Blurbs… In Full ... 125

Contact Details ... 127

CHAPTER 1

Introduction

Jack Blanchard and Misty Morgan – what do these names mean to you? Are you a fan, or have you never heard of them? Whichever side of the fence you fall you will be fascinated by their story – a story of their life as hard-working musicians, knowing hardship and sometimes danger, their rise to fame and fortune during their heyday, right through to their come-back in the digital age, long after many people thought that they had disappeared from the scene forever.

Jack and Misty are forever linked, in so many people's mind, to their huge hit, 'Tennessee Birdwalk', which unexpectedly shot them to fame in 1970. Anyone who was tuned into the radio that spring and summer would have found it difficult to miss this song which reached #1 on the US Billboard country charts in April that year. The song also crossed over to be #23 in the pop charts. It was being played on radio stations all over the USA and in Canada for many months and people were singing it everywhere.

But there is so much more to their story than this song.

Some will recall a few more of their charted songs such as 'Somewhere in Virginia in the Rain', 'There Must Be More To Life (Than Growing Old)' or 'Humphrey The Camel' but, apart from that, not many people know very about much them. This biography will fill in some of the gaps in knowledge about this talented duo, who both started life in Buffalo, NY, and who met many years later in Florida, where they joined forces before getting married in 1963.

Their adventures are so numerous that only a selection of them can be told in this book. They have been through so much over the years, having seen both the highs and the lows of the music business. They have known thrills and bitter disappointments, triumphs and rejections, personal joys and family tragedy, riches and poverty, danger and the kindness of people who helped them when the going got really tough. They have recorded songs for which they never received a penny. They have played gigs for which they did not get paid. They have been robbed, mugged, cheated and stalked.

They have, at least once, thought that their end had come, like the time when, traveling on a road high in the Appalachian mountains, two burst tires nearly tipped them over the edge of the mountainside. They have experienced being made homeless in Miami, when their money wouldn't cover both their rent and the payments on their car. Ill health brought them to the edge of bankruptcy when their insurance would not cover all their medical bills, causing them to lose their home, their furniture and much of everything else that they owned.

By contrast they have performed before crowds of thousands, in huge auditoriums and at numerous festivals, sharing the stage with many of the biggest names in the country music world. Other times they played in tiny clubs, with only a handful of listeners, where no one knew or cared who they were. They have known the generosity of fans and strangers who have helped them when bills were higher than their income, and so many other small acts of kindness.

Between them they have created a unique and distinctive sound. Misty's beautiful alto voice harmonizes perfectly with Jack's deep gravelly voice, which has been described as a 'velvet saw', a description which was the idea of Tom McConnell, promotion manager for Hall-Clement Publications and Mega Records. Jack later took the name 'Velvet Saw' as the name for his own record label. In addition, Misty is Jack's 'straight man', complementing his on-stage comedy.

Some of the numerous awards they have won over the years include a Grammy nomination and the prestigious Billboard Magazine Award for Duet of the Year in 1970, and in 2004 they were inducted into the New York Country Music Hall of Fame.

Although they have played shows in forty-nine of the fifty states of the USA, they have never traveled outside of the United States, apart from childhood visits to Canada and Jack's Dawn Breakers' tour. Nor, during all those years traveling around the States, did they ever get a chance to play in Buffalo together. Once, before they had any hits, they were booked into a fancy restaurant in Buffalo, but when they got there they found that they had been double booked with another band, so they had to settle for dinner there instead.

They finally achieved their wish to play together in the city of their birth when, on October 7th 2010, they were inducted into the Buffalo Music Hall of Fame. Coincidentally, that day was also their 47th wedding anniversary.

CHAPTER 2

Jack's Early Life

The story starts in Buffalo, New York, just a few miles from the Canadian border and the magnificent Niagara Falls. It was a Thursday in early May and, at the Millard Fillmore Hospital, Jack's mother was giving birth to her first child, a boy. She and her husband John named him John Wesley Jr. The date was May 8th 1930. Right from the start he was known as Jack. His sister, Virginia (Ginny), was born two years later and the family was completed with the birth of his second sister, Valerie, born fourteen years after Jack.

Jack spent most of his childhood living in the Elmwood Village area of Buffalo. He recalls most of his childhood as being a happy one. There was always a lot of love and laughter, with plenty of family parties, particularly at Christmas and Thanksgiving. His parents and grandparents loved any excuse to dress up and to play jokes with each other, and they liked to make a big thing of holidays.

His family frequently took holidays in Canada. Early holiday visits were to Crystal Beach, Ontario, to which steamboats shuttled visitors across Lake Erie from Buffalo. There was an amusement park there, which first opened in 1888. Later on, when Jack was in high school, the family had a house at Waverly Beach, Ontario, where they would spend all summer and early fall. They loved it there and hated to leave. His cousin, Donna, who is close in age to Jack, spent a lot of time with his family during these early years and was like another sister to him.

Jack remembers the austerity of living through World War Two, when people couldn't get butter, rubber tires, nylon hosiery or many other everyday things; the time when the buses had plywood stand/sit seats, to carry more workers to defense plants, and when the wartime mindset didn't allow for gray areas – people were either patriots or traitors – because their neighbors' kids were being slaughtered to defend freedom. Stars could be seen hanging in the windows of the families who had lost a son or daughter; sometimes more than one star.

His maternal grandparents lived nearby, so he grew up knowing them well. His grandfather, Clair Blanchard, was an engineer on the Pennsylvania Railroad. He and his wife, Ethel, were very much into keeping up appearances and wanted the neighbors to think that Clair was a businessman, so when he went to work he wore a business suit and carried a briefcase. Inside the briefcase were his work overalls, shirt and cap, and his lunch box.

His paternal grandparents, Frank John and Elizabeth Snowflake, came from the Miamisburg area in Ohio. Frank's parents were German immigrants from Baden-Württemberg in the southwestern part of Germany. Jack never knew them as his grandmother died eight years before he was born and he was only three when his grandfather died. From what his family told him, his grandfather was a professional pianist and music professor; a dignified man, and a natty dresser for the times.

Jack's father, John Wesley, was nicknamed Jody in his younger days. He lived a colorful life, holding down a variety of different jobs and often doing deals of a questionable nature. Times of plenty for the family were interspersed with times of hardship, depending on what John's current deal or job was. One job he held was as the General

Manager of Bell Aircraft in Buffalo. Other business ventures included being President of the Monarch Mortgage Corporation and of the Oklahoma Royalty Corporation.

In his younger days John was said to have been a flamboyant 'jack of all trades', which included owning a gambling ship, and being a prize fighter and a daredevil. He was also an aviator, who had a flying school in Dayton, OH, and he wrote a course on aeronautics. There were rumors that he had some ties to the black market. Jack recalls coming home from school one day and having difficulty opening the front door. When he finally managed to get into the house, he found it knee deep in silver fox furs. A local dignitary and his wife were there, looking through the pelts before choosing which ones to purchase.

For a time, as a result of one of his deals, John owned the gas station which had the largest underground capacity for gasoline in New York State. It received its supply via a pipeline directly from a private railroad siding. The garage was located at Elmwood and Hertel. Although Jack was only young at the time, he recalls that the attendants were dressed like motorcycle cops, wearing boots, britches, and caps. One day a young guy called Nicky, who worked there, managed to set himself and the garage on fire while cleaning out the grease pit with gasoline and a squeegee (against company rules). The squeegee caught a light bulb and the resulting blast blew off part of the garage roof. Jack's father, John, ran down into the flaming grease pit and carried Nicky to safety, but not before Nicky had sustained severe burns.

Apart from being a natural comedian, a trait Jack has inherited, his father also loved cooking. This latter talent, however, has eluded Jack, even though his mother was also an excellent cook. John was also fearless. Once, when the family were being threatened by thugs after he'd sacked a guy with mob connections for being drunk at work, he went downtown and confronted the local mafia boss. The threats ceased from then on.

Jack's mother, Mary Florence, was known as Virginia, or 'Sissy', a nickname she'd been given by her younger brother during her childhood. She had been a tomboy as a child, but she grew up to be a beautiful woman, with flaming red hair. She was very fashion conscious and was always smartly dressed, as well as being a good home maker. She was a fashion model for a time, but she also held down numerous other jobs to help support the family. She was a good artist and went to art college, but she never had the chance to fully develop her artistic skills. Both she and Jack's father had been married before they met, and she was almost ten years younger than her husband.

When Jack was a young boy he liked to climb a tree in the backyard and look at the world from another angle. The second floor of the family house was at eye level from this vantage point. He said he just liked to see things from a different perspective. In those days the streets around the area were lined with huge elm trees. Unfortunately these were all killed when Dutch Elm Disease struck. They have since been replaced by trees that are not susceptible to this devastating disease.

Jack was fortunate to receive a very good education during his early years in school. Though the classes were large, his teachers were excellent. He reckons that by eighth grade he had learned the equivalent of what is now considered to be a college education. There were a lot of gang wars in the city during his high school days. He describes how the scary guys were from Amherst Street. There was an older guy named Red Webster who knocked him around until about the eighth grade, when Jack finally beat him up at the sandlot baseball field. He said, "We seemed to be buddies after that, but I still picked on him occasionally".

He was a Boy Scout, a Tenderfoot, for two or three years. He described himself as a 'lousy' Scout and that the only knot he ever learned to tie was a sheepshank, which he has never had reason to use. Jack jokingly added, "There were no sheep in our neighborhood".

Although he had been an honors student in grammar school, he hated high school. In subjects like algebra and geometry, for which he had no aptitude, his marks dropped dramatically and he started regularly skipping classes. One day, when he was sneaking around the school halls during a skipped class, he heard music coming from the auditorium. When he looked in through the door he saw a bunch of kids gathered around the piano. Somebody was playing what sounded like Jimmy Durante music. The player was a guy, a year or two older than himself, named Johnny Molay. Jack not only liked the music, but he liked all the girls it attracted. He spent the whole of that summer vacation at his grandparents' upright piano teaching himself to play the Durante style, but when he found some old boogie-woogie piano records around the house he switched to playing boogie style.

After a couple of years in high school Jack said that he became a 'screwed up semi-delinquent'. It was around this time that his father started to become ill with a condition resembling Alzheimer's disease and, shortly after that, he was no longer able to work. Because of Jack's irregular attendance at classes he was expelled from more than one school. However he said that he later went on to teach a college course on jazz theory and orchestration.

One summer his parents, concerned about his behavior, thought that sending him with his Uncle Earl on one of his business trips would keep him away from his unruly friends for a while, not realizing that Jack was the ringleader. He liked his Uncle Earl as he had a good sense of humor and always made the family laugh. He was a big man, with an artificial leg which gave him a distinctive limp. They left at dawn in Earl's beat up station wagon, loaded down with horsey gear, blankets, bridles, blinders, medicines, salves, and so on. His uncle allowed Jack to drive much of the time, even though he was under age. They stopped for a beer in a place where everybody knew Earl, and nobody questioned Jack's age.

At the Hamburg Raceway he learned that Earl was a traveling salesman, selling equipment to horse owners on his regular rounds. He didn't seem to care too much about making a profit, but was more than happy socializing. People would often just buy a small item from him as a friendly gesture, or as payment for the fresh jokes and inside news he dispensed.

For reasons known only to Earl, they took the old narrow roads across New York State, traveling through the Catskills, the land of Ichabod Crane and the Headless Horseman. It was an area of spectacular beauty, with early morning mists in every hollow. Outside Saratoga they turned onto a gravel road, going past a 'No Trespassing' sign and continuing up a mountainside to a rambling brick house, the home of Mrs. O'Hagen. She took them for a tour of the ranch, driving for miles without ever leaving her property. Groups of racehorses ran wild there. That evening she drove them to the racetrack in her Cadillac, which she drove with a vengeance, never dimming her lights for oncoming traffic. At the track, naturally, everybody knew and liked Earl. Jack learned something about his uncle during that trip, which he kept secret for many years, until after his uncle's death. Selling horse equipment was not his real job. His real job was as an undercover race detective for the Association.

Jack's childhood and teens were filled with sport, mainly football and baseball, so he was quite a good athlete by the time he reached high school. He already knew some boys from Kenmore High School and, when the football practices started before the start of the fall semester, these boys took him out to the practice session on the first day, even though Jack was not yet enrolled at the school. During the tryouts, the coach had everyone race the length of the field to see who could run. The shoes Jack was wearing were too loose so he kicked them off but, in spite of running in bare feet, he easily beat the rest of the lads. As a result he became the only known freshman to ever make first string on the football team. The coach had noticed his lack of shoes and asked, jokingly, if he was from Kentucky and he called him 'Kentucky' for the whole of that first season. Jack played quarterback for two years, until he left school. In baseball they put him in center field at first, because of a strong throwing arm, but as he could not throw a straight ball, he was made a pitcher instead. Basketball was one game he didn't excel at as he never liked indoor games. He hated the smell and the echoing acoustics of a gym, and to this day he has retained his dislike of gyms.

Another game he recalls playing was street hockey on roller skates, using a ball from a miniature pool table as a puck. In the winter he and his friends went to Delaware Park every non-school hour to play ice hockey under the bridge where, because it was sheltered from the snow by the arches, the ice stayed smooth as glass. They didn't play hockey in school, but he later played a season of semi-pro hockey for the G.O.P. team, sponsored by the Republican Party. They were given uniforms and transportation, and Jack said that was the closest he ever got to being a Republican.

Jack started showing his musical talent early on and his first instrument was a ukulele. The first time he played it in public was at the age of nine, when he sang 'Little Brown Jug' in front of his fourth grade class. A little later his father bought him a Gibson guitar, but Jack showed little interest in playing it at the time as the steel strings hurt his fingers. After he started playing the piano in his early teens, he picked up the skill quickly. By the age of sixteen he had started playing gigs in the local saloons, the only boogie piano player in the area. The room would get rockin' and he sometimes played one song for a half hour non-stop. He got a lot of attention, especially from the girls, which is what motivated him to learn piano in the first place. One of his first piano gigs was at The Anchor Bar, the place where they invented Buffalo Wings.

During these early years Jack played many clubs in Buffalo. Misty's mother was a pianist and a singer in the same area and their paths crossed at least once, at a gig they both attended, but of course he had no idea then that she would become his future mother-in-law. Misty was to later follow in her mother's footsteps, playing piano and singing in those same clubs around the area.

For a time he was a member of a teenage musical trio, where the other two members, Jerry and Ronny Loft, were Mohawk Indians. One summer they took him to the July 4th races at the Six Nations Reservation in Canada. Jerry and Ronny's relatives were the most important people in that area. They ran the General Store, the Post Office, and the funeral parlor, all in one big rambling house. One night, Jerry and Ronny woke Jack during the early hours and took him downstairs to show him something. It was an old pump organ that was worked by pumping the air with a foot pedal. They fetched their own instruments down too, a guitar and bass, and they began quietly jamming by flashlight and candle light, hoping not to wake the rest of the household. Next thing they knew the whole family was there watching and cheering them on. When they finished, about an hour later, someone switched on the lights. Once Jack's eyes adjusted to the light he saw that they were in the funeral parlor, with two dead bodies in the audience. He had been playing boogie on the funeral organ.

Later on Jack, along with three other friends, formed a vocal pop quartet called The Dawnbreakers. The others in the group were Don Fronczak, Buddy Baker and Jim Warne. Jack was now using his grandparents' surname, Blanchard, which was less prone to mispronunciation than his birth name. Don, Buddy and Jim sang the lead vocals and Jack sang harmony vocals, wrote songs and did the arrangements for the group. He had learned how to arrange music from studying books on arranging for orchestras. An early recording they made was a radio commercial for Everybody's Daily, a Polish newspaper. The recording was made, first in English and then in Polish, and it was recorded in the Churchill Tabernacle, which was chosen because of the good echo.

The Dawnbreakers, whose name was changed to The Dawn Breakers by the record company, had their first studio recording session at Howell's Studio in Buffalo. Their first single was 'The Things I Love', an old standard for which Jack wrote the vocal and instrumental arrangements and sang the harmony vocals. This song became a hit record in the Northeast on Coral Records, a major label which was a subsidiary of Decca Records. However, due to an unwise decision by their manager, their success was short lived. He had made the mistake of giving it to the wrong DJ first. He had given it to Herb Knight at WKBW and, as a result, the popular Rock DJ, George 'Hound Dog' Lorenz, refused to play it on his radio station unless they were willing to give him a payola. As Jack and his friends did not have the kind of money he was asking for, 'Hound Dog' never did play their songs. The 'B' side of this Coral single was 'Boy With the Be-Bop Glasses', which was written by Jack. Furthermore, Jack felt greatly hurt when morning radio personality, Clint Buehlman, to whom he had listened all his life, knocked their recording on air.

As a result of the airplay the song received, an agent out of Buffalo, named Harry Ricci, booked them on a Canadian tour, up around the Northern Ontario mining country. Two of the towns they visited were Sudbury and Timmons. Every town had a theater, one of which was a long-closed movie house. For some reason the stage was unusable and they had to do their show from the orchestra pit. At rehearsal on the first day, Jack plugged in his guitar and amp and got an electric shock. The orchestra pit was the lowest point in the building and all the dampness gathered in that part of the cement floor. Plugging in his guitar was almost like "using a toaster in the bathtub". Somebody brought a flattened cardboard box for him to stand on, to break the ground. It worked, and they went ahead with the rehearsal. After the first song the theater manager walked up to him and said, "Sounds great, Jack", and put his hand on Jack's arm. They both got zapped, but lived to tell the tale.

At another theater, for the price of admission, the audience got The Dawn Breakers' show, plus a Jerry Lewis movie. There were no dressing rooms, so they hung a light bulb behind the movie screen and changed there. They could see the movie in reverse on the back of the screen and they could hear the crowd laugh at Jerry Lewis. However, whenever the screen dimmed down, the laughter took on a different tone. With the light bulb shining on the band members, the audience could see them running around in the buff, right through the screen.

Jack's first band gig was playing piano in Harry Brunn's band, 'H. O. Brunn & the Dixieland Jazz Crackers'. Jack was the youngest member of the band. Harry was the ultimate purist who, during rehearsals, would play records by The Original Dixieland Jazz band. This was the band who were recognized as the first jazz band and who released their first recording in 1917. Harry had his band members learn Dixieland's intricate arrangements, including 'Tiger Rage' which changes key four or five times. They were allowed to improvise, but if anyone played a lick that sounded later than 1929, Harry would stop the rehearsal and yell at them. He was a hard taskmaster, but Jack enjoyed his company and learned a lot from him.

Harry lived in an old mansion in Snyder, New York, a suburb of Buffalo, and he drove a Cord, a car which was only made for a few years between 1929 and 1937. Jack described it as the coolest car he'd ever ridden in.

When Jack's dad became ill with a condition similar to Alzheimer's, and could no longer work, the family was forced to split up. His dad went to live with his sister, Bess, in Miamisburg, Ohio, living there until his death a few years later. Jack remembers going with his family to the railway station to see him leave, not knowing if they would ever see him again. Shortly after this, Jack's mother and his two sisters moved to Florida to live with his maternal grandparents, who had moved there a few years earlier. Jack chose to stay on in the Buffalo area. He only saw his dad one more time, a few years later, when he stopped off in Miamisburg while hitchhiking between Florida and Buffalo. His dad recognized him after a few minutes and gave him a big hug.

Jack was living in North Tonawanda during this time. He had a good friend in Tonawanda called Gordon Leeder. Gordon and his wife owned The Star Dry Cleaners across the street from where Jack lived. He enjoyed Gordon's company and they often played pool and went to some club meetings together. One night Gordon committed suicide with a shotgun. Nobody seemed to know why. Jack was a pallbearer at his funeral and, although it happened so many years ago, he has never forgotten him.

For a short time Jack was a military policeman (MP) in the US National Guard in Buffalo. Less than a year later he got in trouble for failing to show up when required and they kicked him out. He was jailed for ten days as an example to others because, as an MP, he was expected to lead by example, setting a higher standard for others to follow.

There weren't many places in Buffalo for a musician to work, except on weekends. In order to make ends meet Jack worked many other jobs, including factory jobs, grave digging, greasing cement mixers, selling encyclopedias, tending bar and building juke boxes. He never fitted in with any of them, bluffing his way through those jobs where he did not know what he was doing. He never went back to any place that he had worked before. Meanwhile, he continued to take weekend piano jobs wherever he could at any of the many taverns around the area.

A couple of years after his mother and sisters moved south to

Florida he married his high school sweetheart, June. June was a year younger than him and she'd been a model pupil at school, the good girl, in contrast to Jack's reputation as a bit of a trouble maker. Throughout his teens Jack was very shy with girls, but June was determined to marry him. She was his first serious sweet-heart. She was also a good singer and pianist, and she could read music, which Jack couldn't do at the time. In the early years of their marriage they frequently played music together. However, as marriage partners, they were not a good match. Though Jack loved June in a teenage way, he was not really ready for the responsibilites of marriage. June, however, was head over heels in love with him and persuaded him that they should get married. When the children, a daughter, Kathi, and a son, Donn, came along, although he loved them very much, he was not able to spend much time with them due to the demands of his music career, which he saw as their only way out of poverty.

After getting into a spot of trouble in a fight, when he broke someone's nose, he moved down to his grandparents' home in Florida. June followed shortly afterwards. The family soon settled in Miami, near the rest of his family. They found work there, but with the children to take care of, June was not able to help Jack with his singing career, and their marriage was starting to break up. Over time, a combination of alcohol, amphetamines, and the increasing time Jack was spending away from home pursuing his music career, led to ever more violent rows between them, and Jack left the family home for good before June knew that she was expecting their second daughter, Michele.

CHAPTER 3

Misty's Early Life

Six years after Jack's birth, on another May day and in the same hospital, Buffalo's Millard Fillmore Hospital, a daughter was born to Rosemary Donahue. It was Saturday 23rd May 1936. Rosemary named her Mary Ann. A few years later she would be joined by a brother, Bob, and later by a sister, Virginia. For the first few years of her life Mary Ann and her mother lived with her grandfather, William Donahue. William would have had Irish ancestors, as Donahue is the Americanized version of an Irish surname. Misty could trace other ancestors to the Alsace-Lorraine region of Europe and she believes that she also has some Native American blood.

[It wasn't until the late 1960's that Mary Ann (a.k.a. Maryanne) took the name Misty, a name chosen for her by Jack. However, for clarity, she will be referred to as Misty in the following pages.]

When she was about four years old her mother married John Griffin. Shortly afterwards, her grandfather died. She was known throughout most of her childhood as Mary Ann Griffin, having taken her stepfather's surname, though she was never officially adopted by him.

She had a hard childhood, with a difficult relationship with her mother. Much of the time she barely had enough to eat or enough clothes to wear. Later on in her life, due to some confusion about her real surname, she lost out on an inheritance she should have received from her grandfather. Some of this money was to have paid for her to go to the Eastman School of Music. Instead, her mother, with the collusion of the administrator of her grandfather's estate, had already spent most of the money. Misty only found out about what her mother had been doing after it was too late for her to do anything about it. By then most of the money was spent and the house that Misty should have inherited had been put into her mother's name.

She was brought up as a Catholic and, for a time during her childhood, she attended St. Joseph's church on Main Street, Buffalo. Family photos include one of her taken just after her first communion. There is also a photo of her as a thirteen year old, enjoying a trip in a small boat on Lake Erie with her step-father and her aunt, for whom she had a special affection.

She hated school, leaving Tonawanda High School, near Buffalo, as soon as she was able to. She had only been at this school for a year or two before she quit to go into music. Years later an old school friend, Myna, wrote to her, reminding her about the time when there was a fire on Niagara Street and they had stood watching the blaze together.

Misty has always loved animals and she had a number of pets during her childhood, including a raccoon which she was very fond of. She was particularly fond of dogs and owned many in the years to come.

Her mother had taught her to play the piano, starting when she was about five. Misty took a few piano lessons as a child, but her teachers kept quitting because she wouldn't play what was on the sheet music. Instead she played something she liked better.

By the time she was fourteen she was following in her mother's footsteps, playing piano and singing in the bars and combos around

Tonawanda. She was playing standards, dance music, Broadway, popular songs of the day and a little country music. She couldn't read music, but she was fortunate to have inherited the gift of being able to play any tune after having heard it just once, and her beautiful alto voice complemented her piano playing. Apart from playing piano, Misty also did some tap dancing in her youth. She could have gone into circus life as she had a distant cousin, Kitty Irwin, who was an acrobat and trapeze artist, but she chose music instead.

When she was sixteen her mother threw her out of the house in the middle of winter. Her sister wanted to come with her, but she was too young. Shortly after, Misty ran off to Catlettsburg, Kentucky with Brian Male, whom she had known for a while. They got married there, returning to Buffalo for a time before moving to Cincinnati, Ohio, seeking better work prospects. While in Cincinnati, Misty played piano at a club owned by the parents of Doris Day. During the day Misty supplemented their income by working as a stenographer with a lithography company. A couple of years later, her daughter, Susan, was born.

Following a car accident, which was not their fault, she and Brian were being sued by the other driver. He was a millionaire with a lot of local clout and they were about to lose their home, so they left town and headed south to Florida, where job prospects looked better.

It was not a happy marriage and Misty suffered a lot of violence from Brian. They scraped by, with Misty working various day jobs; waitressing, car hopping and a variety of other jobs, while playing clubs in the evenings. Brian was often without work and they were living in an old trailer with minimal facilities. She had to leave her baby daughter with child minders while she worked.

By the time Susan was two, Misty had had enough of her husband's abusive behavior and she left him, taking her daughter with her. She feared for her daughter's safety, as well as her own. As soon as Brian discovered she had gone, he followed her, and burned her car and all her belongings, including all the photos she had of Susan as a baby. In order to support herself and her young daughter, Misty was having to work more than one job at a time, as well as playing in clubs in the evenings.

For a while she worked in a veterinarian's office and she recalls the day that a lady called in, bringing with her a pet lion. She wanted to leave the lion for a short time while she was going to be away from home. Fortunately the lion was very tame and gentle, as Misty had the job of taking it for walks on a lead round the compound. She said that its paws were huge. She was sorry when the lion had to be returned to its home a short time later.

By now Jack & Misty were both working in Hollywood, Miami, having arrived in Florida at roughly the same time as each other. They became aware of each other's existence as they were both playing clubs in the same area, and their names and pictures were often in the local papers and on posters and club billboards round the town. When they finally met, Misty was playing, under the name Mary Male, with a country band, 'Two Kings and a Queen', at The Corral Barbecue in West Hollywood, Florida. By this time she was divorced and Jack was separated from his wife.

After Misty and Jack had been together for a couple of years, they read in The Miami Herald that Brian had been found murdered in an unrented room at the Voyager Motel, on US 1 in North Miami Beach. He had been shot and, when he was found, he was still clutching handfuls of rare coins. They have no idea why he was murdered, nor of the significance of the coins he was found holding. It is a mystery that will probably never be solved.

CHAPTER 4

Starting Out Together

The first time that Jack saw Misty she was playing with her band at the Coral Club in West Hollywood. He was attracted to her at first sight. He wanted to get to know her better, so he invited her to meet him at an after hours place they both knew. When he got there, he was told that she just left. It seems that her friends had told her that Jack was a mob guy and, after arriving at the venue she got cold feet, so she left again before Jack arrived. In fact Jack wasn't part of the mob, but he did work in clubs owned by them, playing piano for them on and off. As his dress and bearing fitted in with his working lifestyle, people seeing him thought that he looked the part. Indeed, for quite some time, he was friends with one notorious gangster in Miami, who treated him like a son. As Jack had not known who this man was when they first met, he had no preconceived attitudes toward him. He just seemed to be a nice old man. Later, when he learned about this man's bloody and violent career, Jack was unable to turn off the friendship, and everything he read about him in the newspapers seemed as if they were writing about somebody else. Quite apart from all this, following her previous traumatic experience of marriage, Misty didn't feel ready to risk getting into another relationship.

Several weeks passed before their paths crossed again. This time they met at a benefit gig, where they both got up and played. They started to hit it off that night and Misty ditched the guy she came with and left with Jack. They went for a midnight breakfast at a local restaurant, but afterwards they just said goodnight and went their separate ways. Jack said he was wary of pushing too hard in case he frightened her off and he wanted to see her again. Misty said later that she had been hoping Jack would give her a goodnight kiss, but he didn't – not that night anyway.

They ran into each other once or twice more over the following months. Then one evening, on his night off, Jack stopped by at the Copa Lounge and found Misty talking to his boss. They both laughed about her trying for his job, but this was the turning point in their romance. Jack says he did kiss her that night – more than once. They began seeing a lot of each other after that and, soon after, they began playing music together, sometimes as a duo, sometimes as a trio.

They had only been together for a short time when, one evening, they went to a club to hear an all-female jazz quintet. Somebody asked Misty to sit in on piano and she accepted the invitation. Jack was embarrassed, as he didn't think Misty could play jazz. He turned to her and said, "Honey, you don't play jazz". She just replied, "I can do it".

As she went on-stage he went to the rest room, as he didn't want to see her make a fool of herself. Then he heard this great jazz piano, a mix of Oscar Petersen, Erroll Garner and Ramsey Lewis. He went out and looked and, to his surprise, it was Misty. She brought the house down. He said to her, "Where the hell did you learn that?" She just calmly said, "I told you I could do it". He hadn't realized until then that, as well as having a beautiful voice, Misty had the gift of being able to play any tune by ear after hearing it just once.

They had some very lean times during their early years together and, at one point, they were made homeless when they didn't have enough money to pay both their rent and the payments on their car.

They chose to make the car payment, but then the car was impounded by the finance company because they didn't have an address after being evicted for not paying the rent. A couple of days later, Jack's mother managed to give them enough money from her limited income for them to rent a run-down room in a slum neighborhood, where they stayed until they found work again. Having an address again enabled them to get the car and their belongings back, but the landlord would put a padlock on their room door whenever they were even an hour late with the weekly rent. They were glad when they were able to move from there.

Soon after, Jack joined a rhythm and blues band which was working at a mob owned club, the 'King O' Hearts Club', on NW 7th Avenue in Miami. Misty had noticed an ad in a local paper for a bass player and she persuaded him to apply. He was reluctant at first because it was a union club and he wasn't a union member. Neither was he a bass player. However Misty insisted and wouldn't leave him alone until he agreed to try for it. He auditioned, and they took him on anyway, playing bass on the keyboards. He rejoined the union while working there.

The band at this club was called 'Donel Austin and the Rockin' Impallas'. The band members were Donel Austin, lead vocalist and rhythm guitar; Doug Tarrant, lead guitar; Frank Kennedy on drums; and Jack, on piano, organ, and left hand bass. The club was like an airplane hangar. The band faced a long oval shaped bar and Donel would often jump from the bandstand and walk along the top of the bar, while belting out his songs. Behind the bandstand there was a giant concrete dance floor. Jack worked behind the piano at the back of the stage, with a big drop behind him if he stepped back.

A live radio show was broadcast every night from the club and, one evening, an argument broke out while they were on air. It turned into a fistfight. In the ensuing melee Jack's piano, which was balanced on top of whiskey cases so that he could play standing up, started to topple over. Jack was straining every muscle, trying to hold it up with his bare hands, while looking at the drop to the cement floor behind him. Just then someone yelled at him, "Keep playing, kid! We're on the air!"

It was a rough venue, but the music was good. They sounded very like a black band, and black people would hear them on the radio and come along to the club, hoping to see them live. However segregation was still in force, so they were refused admission. Jack hated this policy, but he needed the work at the time. A little while later, the band got a higher paying job at another club, 'The Club Seventeen'. However the owner of the 'King O' Hearts' sent his bouncers round to the new club and intimidated the customers and the band until they went back to work at the 'King O' Hearts', under duress.

Hoping to flatter the club owners, Jack wrote a song titled 'King O' Hearts'. He later recorded this with the band, now renamed on the record label as 'Jackie Blanchard and the Rockin' Impallas'. The flip side was 'Only A Fool'. He also made some recordings with Misty, under the names Maryanne Mail and Jacqueline Hyde. On some of these recordings she was supported by Paul Gale, whose real name was Paul McLaughlin, on tenor sax. As Maryanne Mail, she also recorded a couple of duets with Rusty Diamond.

Rusty was a singer with a talent for finding rich girlfriends, who he could persuade to back his music, using their money to pay for studio time and to buy expensive outfits for himself and his backing bands. One song he recorded, with Misty singing harmony, was 'The Lonely Sentry', which was later released on the Starday album, 'Country Music Goes To War'. On this recording Jack was on piano. In addition, an electric pedal banjo (an instrument invented and played by Henry Cook) and church bells were added for effect. Jack said afterwards, "It was probably the best country record ever made in Florida". This was the first song to be recorded that featured both Jack and Misty playing together.

During the time when they were recording with Starday, Jack was friends with a publisher named Bob Montgomery. Jack showed him a song called 'Pass Around the Apples', which Bob thought Norma Jean might cut. He promised Jack that he would return the publishing rights to him within six weeks if Norma didn't want it. After a year, with no promised cut, Jack reminded Bob of his promise, but Bob just asked his lawyers to tell Jack that they weren't going to return the rights. The next time Jack approached him, about publishing another song, he got the cold shoulder. He never knew why Bob's attitude towards him changed the way it did. That first song never did get recorded as, by that time, Jack had forgotten how it went and he hadn't retained a copy of it. Another artist who was associated with Starday Records at that time was Willie Nelson but, much as Jack and Misty would have liked to have met him, they never did.

Some time later Donel Austin and Jack wrote some songs together. Recordings of those songs can now be found at The Rockabilly Hall of Fame.

During the mid sixties, Misty's on-stage show consisted of more jazz-oriented stuff, like Louis Prima and Keely Smith did in the 50's. She could play all kinds of music but, as she did not read music, she never played any tune the same way twice. However, to Jack's knowledge, she was the first female entertainer ever to play six stacked keyboards on stage.

During their first year playing together they played at the Downtowner in Key West. They were starting to experiment with various electronic adaptations to the keyboards, some of which they rented from other musicians until they could afford their own. They were also using a little crystal mike, like a CB radio microphone, as that was all they could afford at the time. They paid about $15 for it at a radio store. Even so, Jack says, it sounded pretty good – "like an old fashioned dial telephone". They continued to experiment and innovate with their music in years to come.

Sometimes they played as the Jack Blanchard trio, when master guitarist, Doug Tarrant, joined them. At the time Doug was playing his original Les Paul model guitar, getting the latest techno sound with an Echofonic, which was probably the first tape echo device ever marketed for live performance. They were already setting new trends. They played a variety of music, including rock & roll, jazz, standards, and current hits, and they loved the music of Les Paul and Mary Ford. This was all quite some time before Jack and Misty ever thought of singing duets together on stage.

By now they were starting to get gigs further afield and, in the autumn of 1963, they were on their way to a gig in South Carolina when Jack pulled over, just after they crossed the border from Florida into Georgia, stopping at the small town of Kingsland. Doug and his wife, Sundee, were traveling with them. When they asked Jack why he had stopped, he told them that he and Misty were getting married. They went to the local court house, paid the necessary fees for the marriage license, and Doug and Sundee acted as their witnesses. Jack's divorce had only just been finalized and the decision to get married was so 'spur of the moment' that Jack did not even have a ring for Misty, so he had to borrow one for the ceremony. The date was October 7th 1963.

In 1965 they recorded their first instrumental together. It was called 'Gemini'. Jack produced the recording at Criteria Studios in Miami, with five musicians, including Misty. The recording was done for under $500. It was soon getting a lot of airplay and was starting to become a hit. They often listened for it on the radio. One day they were in their car, with the radio playing, when it came on. Part way through they suddenly looked at each other and said, "We don't change key there". They then realized that The Ventures had recorded a cover version of it and, as the DJs gave preferential airplay to the better known group, it killed Jack & Misty's version.

Soon after, local singers began asking Jack to produce records for them. They paid him a small fee, plus expenses, to go Nashville for the sessions, and this gave him the chance to get a foot in the door in Music City. Before this, he and Misty had never played country music together.

During another lean period Jack was playing piano at the Last Chance Bar, on US 1 in Florida City, the last saloon on the United States mainland. He had canvassed every bar up and down US 1 before arriving at this one. He bought a beer and just sat down and started playing, mostly boogie and blues, which the few customers there seemed to like. He was given a regular job there. The salary was low, but the tips were pretty good.

Meanwhile, Misty had picked up a gig at the Redland Tavern, a couple of towns away. The job called for someone who could play the Hammond organ. As she and Jack were broke, she told her Miami Beach agent that she could play it. She spent about half an hour trying to work out how to play it before confessing to the owner that she didn't even know how to turn it on. However they had a piano, with an Organo attachment, at the side of the room and she was allowed to play that instead. The owners were nice people and, as she was a good pianist, they kept her on.

Now that they were both working, they went out and, though it was stretching their budget, they rented a small house in Homestead. The house had a screened in front porch. From the street people could look in the windows, seeing right through the living room and into the kitchen. One evening, on their night off, they were both in the kitchen. Misty was standing by the stove and sink and was visible from the street. Jack was sitting at the table, to the right of the kitchen door, and could not be seen. They heard the porch screen door creaking slowly open.

They looked at each other and Jack raised a hand, signaling her to stay where she was, while he sneaked silently, in a half crouch, through the living room to the front inside door. They could hear the screen door still opening. Jack threw open the front door, jumped onto the porch and slammed the screen door, catching the guy's arm in it, preventing his escape. He asked him what he wanted. "Food", was the reply. However they suspected that he was really more interested in assaulting Misty. Misty came into the living room and shouted, "You hold him and I'll go get the 45". Jack replied, "Go! I'm gonna blow his head off!" They didn't have a gun, but the intruder didn't know that. He took off like a shot, leaving his sleeve in the door.

By renting this house, they had taken on more than they bargained for as they had forgotten to take the utility bills and other regular expenses into their calculations. They were worried. One evening Jack went to work as usual at the Last Chance. The bartender, who was also an NCO at the Air Force base in Homestead, told Jack that he was exhausted and needed a night off. Jack offered to take his place on a Sunday night, his night off. When asked if he could tend bar, he lied and said, "Sure. No problem". He knew that the electric bill was overdue, and he and Misty were desperate for money.

The following Sunday, Jack learned how to tend bar on the job. During the evening a man came in, who looked even more depressed than Jack felt, and they got talking. The man told Jack that everything he touched turned to money. He was rich, but he had family problems that were getting to him. Jack said to him, "You should be in my place. My wife and I are about to get our power shut off and get evicted". The man replied saying that he could give Jack the money, but that it wouldn't make him happy, as money never does. Jack told him that they were desperate and the man wrote him out a check for $120, worth three or four times what it would be all these years later. The check was on a Key West bank and Jack worried for several days, until it cleared. He never told the regular bartender about the huge tip. He never saw the rich man again, but heard that he owned a major string of truck stops.

Later, after Jack & Misty formed their own group, they started getting plenty of work. They had got a steady job, leading the band at a high class Coral Gables supper club that attracted celebrities. They were playing light jazz dance music, and occasionally slipping in one of their own songs. Larry King was a regular there, and other regulars they got to meet were Gordon McRae, Dobie Gillis' brother, and Vivian Vance's husband. Another regular customer was Richard Nixon. Often, when he came in, Nixon would set a beer on the piano, sit down on the bench, and play for them. When Jack told him that his playing was pretty good, he replied, "Not bad for an ex-politician". This was before Nixon became president.

However, in spite of having a regular job playing at this club, Jack and Misty felt they weren't getting anywhere. One day Dick Gillespie, an Emmy-winning TV producer, came in. Dick owned a local country station, and he had won his Emmy for producing the Colgate Comedy Hour on TV. He and Jack got talking and Jack asked him why, even though they were good musicians, had he and Misty been unable to get a record deal. Dick told them that it was because their style wasn't salable. He told them to go and develop a recognizable style, to get a new image and to write some original material. They should then go to another town and try it out. No matter how self-conscious they might feel about their new look and sound, he said that they should just go ahead, as if they had been that way all along. He said that they would be accepted in a strange town, even though their home town audiences probably wouldn't take to their new image.

They took all his suggestions to heart. They changed their style of clothing and their hairstyles. They started to develop their distinctive harmonies and wrote some new songs. Once they were ready, they got a gig in Key West to try out their new image. Misty had only just started using the new stage name that Jack had chosen for her and, initially, she was having trouble responding to it. The name Misty came from the Erroll Garner hit song of the same name and the surname, Morgan, was chosen just because it sounded good with it.

To their surprise, the place was packed out every night and in about three weeks they had backers and, shortly after, a recording deal. Neither of them could believe the change in their fortunes, but this is how the 'Jack Blanchard & Misty Morgan' duo, that the world came to know and love, was born.

Over the years, many people have remarked about Misty's unusual harmonies. Jack claims he has no idea what she's doing and that he doesn't want to know – he is just happy it works. One thing that makes their sound distinctive is that Misty often sings the harmony part in a lower range than female singers usually do. Also, rather than just singing harmony, she creates a melody of her own that works as harmony. Also they sometimes switch who sings the melody for part of the song. The result gives them the easily recognizable sound loved by their fans.

Their first recording session as 'Jack Blanchard & Misty Morgan' was at Woodland Studios, Nashville in 1967. The first song recorded was 'Bethlehem Steel', which was initially on their own 'Darn Records' label. This song, along with three others, was put on a 45 EP record which was sent to various radio stations.

'Bethlehem Steel' was released as their first single and it started getting local airplay in Florida. A DJ, named Lee ('Hoss') Moss, liked it and called Wayside Records, a New England country label that was starting to get known, and they signed Jack & Misty. This song got a 'Pick' in Billboard, which meant it was considered to be among the new releases that had a good chance of becoming a hit, but it failed to make the main charts. Their second Wayside single, 'Big Black Bird', got a 'Top 10 Pick' in Billboard, not on the country charts, but on the pop charts. Billboard just didn't know what genre to put Jack & Misty in. This song started to get heavy airplay and Wayside was afraid it would get too big for them, so they made a distribution deal with Mercury/Smash Records. Regrettably, they argued so long about the terms of the deal that the single had to be re-released, by which time it had lost much of its momentum and newness.

In addition to his music, Jack also had a part-time role as a newspaper columnist. It was in this role that he attended the Disney World groundbreaking ceremony in 1967. He was, however, not impressed with the press conference that he was invited to attend.

CHAPTER 5

Hitting the Big Time

After ten years or more of living more or less hand to mouth, and being made homeless on at least one occasion, the start of the seventies was a complete contrast. At last, Jack and Misty had gotten their big break. Some while earlier they had recorded a song called 'Tennessee Birdwalk', which was released on the Wayside/Smash label. Jack and Misty had written this song in about twenty minutes, just for a bit of fun.

It was late on a Friday night, as they were nearing the end of the recording session. The musicians, who were tired after a long week, were getting ready to pack up when Misty said, "Hold on, we have one more song to do". Even though they were tired, once they got started, the musicians loved it. It took one quick run through and one take, and the job was done. It was nearly 1am when they finished. Jack tried to persuade the record company not to release it, as he was afraid that they'd be branded as a novelty act. Fortunately for everyone concerned, he was overruled. The song was released and began to climb the charts.

It started getting airplay on WABC New York which, at the time, was the most listened-to clear-channel, top 40, music signal in the United States. 'Cousin Brucie' Morrow, the number one DJ in the U.S., was on and was heard playing 'Tennessee Bird Walk' back to back, and telling his listeners that this was the "hit to watch".

By early April 1970 it had reached the #1 spot on the country charts, where it remained for two weeks. It also reached #23 on the pop charts, and stayed in the charts for 16 weeks. Jack and Misty could not believe their change of fortune. After all their years of struggling they had finally made it. Everywhere they went people were singing their song. With this recording, Misty also became the first woman to co-produce a #1 country song.

On 4th April 1970 they were invited to appear on the Grand Ole Opry, along with Jack Green, Jeanie Seeley, Wilma Lee and Stony Cooper, Ernie Ashworth, Leroy Van Dyke, Ernest Tubb, Grandpa Jones, Bill Anderson, Marty Robbins, Archie Campbell, Stringbean, Jim & Jessie, Stu Phillips, Snuffy Miller and other artists. It was a memorable occasion and they kept a copy of the cast list for that evening.

Their record company wanted a similar follow-on song to 'Tennessee Bird Walk', so they wrote and recorded 'Humphrey the Camel' which charted at #5. When this song became popular, the Beanie Baby doll company made and marketed a doll named 'Humphrey the Camel'. As so often happens in the music business, Jack and Misty never got paid for the use of the name, nor were they even mentioned by the company.

Their third hit, at #27, was 'You've Got Your Troubles (I've Got Mine)', a song written by UK songwriters, Roger Cook and Roger Greenaway, and first recorded by The Fortunes. This was one of the few covers that they recorded.

The December after getting their big hit, they treated themselves to a special Christmas gift, a new Corvette. They were very proud of that car, on the sides of which they had their 'Birdwalk' logo emblazoned. People all around their home area soon recognized them coming. While they were away touring they would sometimes ask a friend to take it for a run occasionally, to make sure that the battery didn't go flat. Their friend often took Jack's sister, Ginny, with him on these trips. Ginny loved it when people mistook them for Jack and Misty, waving to them and cheering as they went by. A photo of this car was used on their 'Tennessee Birdwalk' sheet music.

Jack & Misty were among the first innovators in country music. They constantly added new and different sounds, and experimented with instrumentation, rhythms and story lines. They were the first major country act to use analog synthesizers, similar to the Moog. They have always liked to write and record the music that they enjoyed, and they just hoped that the public would like it too. They reckoned that their listeners could hear the fun they were having in their studio sessions. They liked to have all the pickers and singers in the studio at the same time, like a party. That way they inspired each other. Overdubs were a rarity. They kept on pushing the envelope, but gently, so as not to alienate their audience by becoming too extreme. There are some people who have never forgiven them for using a Wah-Wah pedal on 'Tennessee Birdwalk'. So popular was this song that many other singers covered it. These included Buck Owens and Susan Raye, Rolfe Harris, Sheb Wooley a.k.a. Ben Colder, The Tennessee Guitars, Living Brass, Henry Mancini, Des O'Connor and Frank Ifield, to name just a few. Sheb Wooley, as he liked to do with many hit songs, also recorded a parody of the song titled 'Tennessee Bird Talk', which he co-wrote with Jack.

While Jack and Misty were with Mercury there were several other, now well-known, artists on the same label. Among them were Tom T. Hall, Jerry Lee Lewis, Faron Young and Roger Miller. Tom T. had the same manager / agent as them for a couple of years, The Bob Neal Agency. Bob Neal was the agent for a lot of stars and they all enjoyed socializing at times. When Tom T. needed liner notes for one of his albums, he asked Jack to write them. Jack asked him what sort of thing he would like written and Tom told him to "write like you usually do". Jack duly obliged, with his own inimitable humor.

You can read what he wrote in chapter 9 of this book.

Their very first job after hearing that they had a number one record was a disaster in many ways, but they found it a little funnier looking back at it. They were booked to appear as guests of Jimmy Dean for five consecutive nights in Salt Lake City – just Jimmy, with a full orchestra, and Jack and Misty with their small band. It is usual for acts to arrive at a venue with their band hours ahead of the show's start time, giving them time to set up all the equipment, tune up and run through a song or two to get the sound right. When they and their band arrived at the venue they were tired, but excited. They hadn't yet had time to buy a bus or motor home, and the five of them had traveled cross-country in a Ford station wagon, towing a U-haul trailer full of their stuff. They got ready to unload all their equipment, including a full size organ.

Jimmy Dean was friendly and funny. They liked him right away. He sent a big bouquet of flowers to Misty in their dressing room, and being a fan, she got an autographed picture from him. However, when they went to set up their equipment, they were confused to find that the stage was round, and that it rotated while they were on it. Jimmy Dean's manager was there. He was most unhelpful and, because of his attitude, Jack nicknamed him 'Bob Hitler'. Jack asked him what part of the stage they were supposed to set up on and he said, "You can't set up before the show. Jimmy uses the whole stage". Jack asked if they could work from the orchestra pit below the stage edge, but 'Bob Hitler' told him that it would be occupied by an orchestra. When Jack explained that they needed about an hour to set up and get a sound check, he was told that they would have to cut that time down to a couple of minutes, run on stage after their introduction, and set up in front of the crowd before they could start their act. Jack was fuming and felt like murdering the guy, but it was too late to go nearly 2,500 miles back home.

They watched Jimmy Dean from the backstage passageway entrance and thought he was terrific. He had the audience in stitches with his jokes and the music was beautiful, backed by his 18 piece band, complete with strings. At the end of his set he gave Jack and Misty a nice buildup and they, and their band members, ran on stage as best they could, weighed down carrying amps, microphones, stands, wires, drums and other instruments. They then went back for the organ, which felt like it weighed two tons. For what felt like eternity, they were crawling around on the floor, plugging things in. The silence got pretty uncomfortable, both for them and the crowd – a packed house. Once they got their mikes working, Jack tried to think of something to say while the guys finished the setup. He said "Isn't Jimmy Dean great?" It was a bad idea. According to 'Bob Hitler', Jack had committed the cardinal sin of show business. He shouted, "You should NEVER say a word to the audience before at least two songs!" According to Jack, he actually said the exclamation point.

Once they finally got started, the crowd loved them. During the show they sang mostly their own songs, closing with 'Tennessee Birdwalk', and Jack told the people stories, bringing them into the music. Their musicians, on lead guitar, sax, and drums, were some of the best around. Jack played rhythm twelve-string guitar and did most of the talking. They had a fine, if unusual show, one they had been doing for a long time, while paying their dues. When their show finished, the crowd gave them a standing ovation. This was only slightly marred by their efforts to try to find their way off that rotating stage. To add to the fun Misty, who played left-foot bass on the organ and worked with one boot off, was limping, with one boot on and the other in her hand, while they were wandering around trying to find where to get off the stage.

It seemed that 'Bob Hitler' was jealous of the response they received because he told their manager and agent that they needed more experience. It could have been that his refusal to let them set up before Jimmy Dean's set was a deliberate ploy to show them up in a bad light, as he obviously didn't want them to outshine Jimmy.

As a result of his comments to their manager and agent, Jack & Misty were given bookings "running all over the map" for a whole year – at a cheap rate. During this time they were paid barely enough to cover their band's wages and their traveling expenses, leaving them next to nothing for their own needs.

After having three hits in quick succession, their record company wanted to bring in their own house producer. Jack resisted as he didn't want the sound that he and Misty had put so much effort into developing to be changed. As a result, the company refused to release any more of the songs that they had recorded. It would be another two years before they were freed from that contract, during which time they were unable to sign up with another company. This meant that they lost a lot of their momentum. They did eventually sign with another company and had a further twelve charted songs on Billboard, but never again in the top ten, even though they recorded several other potential hits. Indeed, according to the charts in Cashbox and Record World, the other main trade publications, they had 18 or 20 hits.

Then their career was dealt another blow when the label that had released their big hits of the past year went bankrupt. An album had been released about the same time as 'Humphrey The Camel', titled 'Birds Of A Feather'. It hit #16 on the country album charts (and #185 on the Pop charts), yet Jack and Misty never saw a penny from royalties on either the album or the singles.

In Nashville, during the early seventies, Jack and Misty's friend, publisher and acting manager was Bill Hall. The role of publishers, which used to be primarily producing sheet music, had changed during the previous forty years. Now their main role was to help artists and writers with their careers, making deals, introducing them to important people, getting recording contracts and finding good agents for bookings. Bill was a publisher who took a personal interest in the artists on his books and he did more of those things than many other publishers. Some of the other people under Bill's wing at this time were Jerry Foster, Bill Rice, Bob McDill, Wayland Holyfield and Dickie Lee. Jerry Foster and Bill Rice co-wrote a beautiful song for Jack and Misty called 'I Will', which they later recorded. Bill Hall was the brother-in-law of Misty's friend, Jan Dyer (co-writer of Kenny Rogers & Dotty West's hit 'Every Time Two Fools Collide'). Misty recalls the day that Bill sent Jan out to buy Christmas wine for all the writers in the office. She went with Jan to get the wine and they then went on to a beautiful, big, white house. They were seated in front of the fireplace with Jan's friend, Larry Butler, and Jan introduced them. They were talking about United Artists, who Larry was working for at the time, when Larry told Misty how much he liked their music. This introduction led to Jack and Misty being hired by United Artists.

As well as being their partner in Birdwalk Music Publications, Bill was also the business partner of Cowboy Jack Clement, the legendary producer and songwriter, whose career had started at Sun Studios in Memphis, the studios owned by Sam Philips. While there, Cowboy Jack had worked with the likes of Elvis Presley, Roy Orbison, Carl Perkins, Johnny Cash, Charlie Rich and Jerry Lee Lewis. Later on, after he moved to Nashville, he discovered Charley Pride and was responsible for persuading Chet Atkins to sign him to RCA. While Jack and Misty worked with Bill, they worked in the same building as Cowboy Jack for a couple of years, but they didn't get to meet him face to face until they visited Nashville again years later, in 2011. Bill once told Jack that somewhere around 95% of all number one hits are love songs. Jack reckoned that Bill was trying to get him off his unorthodox song writing subjects, such as birds in dirty underwear, robbery and murder in a dark old city, a guy being buried who seemed to know what was going on, a country singer falling in love with a fire hydrant and songs about birth, death, and beyond. Needless to say, though Jack did go on to write some beautiful love songs, he continued to write about unusual subjects.

During the time when Jack was trying to figure how his voice, and the way he wrote songs, would fit into the country music business, he said that Roger Miller was a great help to him. Roger's voice and style of writing were in the same category as Jack's, in that neither fitted the commonly accepted Nashville mold. Neither he, nor Roger, believed in putting a fence around country music. When Roger wrote, every word and every phrase in his songs added something to the whole, with no fill ins. Jack sought to follow his example in his own songwriting – any word that didn't add something, erase it. He said that he learned a lot from Roger. As a result, some of Jack's early country songs had a strong Miller influence and, although most people didn't hear it, Jack was very aware of it. Jack was, and still is, a Roger Miller fan. He recalled the day when Misty and he were doing a session at Columbia's Studio B. Roger's session in studio A was already going on. They took a few minutes to watch him at work through the window in the door and Jack remembered hearing Roger say over the microphone, "Let's go, folks. We're losin' light". A little later, right in the middle of their own session, Roger walked in, carrying a brief case, and stood by the door listening. Jack stopped everything, telling Misty that he had to go meet Roger and tell him what a big fan he was. Just as he approached Roger with his hand out, Roger said, "Hi, Jack. I'm a fan of yours". Jack said that this was one of the best moments of his life.

A long train journey from Orlando to Pittsburgh sticks in their minds. It was late winter and they were on their way to do a national television show for a PBS station in Pittsburgh, before going on to Nashville for a recording session. They settled down in their compartment and stowed their luggage. They heard an official voice inviting them to the dining car for the hospitality hour and Misty said, "Let's live a little". They made their way forward, weaving with the sway of the train. As they passed through the club car, the train rounded a curve, and Misty lost her balance and sat on a man's lap. His wife was not amused. In the dining car they watched the scenery fly by. They stayed awake most of that night, wiping the steam from their breath off the train window, and watching the sparkling towns and moonlit woodlands fall away behind them. They left this luxury train in Washington and boarded a coach bound for Pittsburgh, which wove slowly through the gray land of Appalachia. Everything was drab from the smoky air, which left its film on town and country alike, dulling the colors, and there were dingy crusts of snow and slush lying around. A gang of workmen, who were lined up in the aisle waiting to get off the train to go home after a hard days work, whispered and snickered at their haircuts and clothes. The hospitality of the staff on the train was much appreciated, bringing color back to this leg of the journey. Before long, they were greeted by the sight of a beautiful, rocky river, which wandered for miles through scenic hill country. It was a memorable journey.

Jack had always wanted to visit Hollywood, California, and they got the chance when Mercury Records set up a deal for him and Misty to be on the Lawrence Welk TV Show. Jack couldn't see how they would fit on that show, and he was right. Welk's producer took one look at them and backed out of the deal. Instead he had another duo, Guy and Ralna, sing 'Tennessee Birdwalk' on the show. Their friends at Mercury saved the day by booking them on two other shows, Dick Clark's American Bandstand and The Robert W. Morgan Show. Afterwards they spent a lot of time hanging out with Dick Clark. One day Jack told him, "You really are a nice guy" and Dick replied, "That's all I've got going". They had asked to stay at the legendary, but rundown, Hollywood Plaza Hotel at Hollywood and Vine. However, by the time they got there, it seemed like a retirement home for old actors, with all the familiar faces sitting around the lobby. When the air conditioner in their room stopped working, they called the front desk. The man who came up to look at it was Maxie Rosenbloom, the great comic character actor and ex-boxer. At the Robert W. Morgan Show they got lost backstage and wandered into Tina Turner's dressing room by mistake. What did Tina do in response to the intrusion? She started singing 'Tennessee Birdwalk'. It gave them all a good laugh.

Sometime around 1973, Jack and Misty's tour bus broke down in Valdosta, Georgia. While they were waiting for the bus to be fixed, Jack called the local country music station (WJEM) and talked to the DJ, Gary Monroe, whom he knew from previous phone conversations. Gary, who's real name is Gary Graves, arranged to meet them at his house, where he introduced them to Joel Mathis, a talented local country singer. Gary's wife, Ann, and their kids were there too. Somebody handed Jack a flat top guitar. Gary set up a mike and a tape recorder, and Jack pitched some of his songs to Joel. A while later, Joel recorded three of those songs and Jack produced the session for him in Nashville.

Twenty-five years or more later, right out of the blue, Jack received a CD from Gary in the mail. Shortly before this, Jack had been remastering some recordings of Joel's music for Gary, including the three songs that Jack had written. On that CD was an hour or more of the recordings that Gary had made that day, when Jack was pitching his songs to Joel, all those years ago. Snippets of conversation and the voices of Gary's kids can be heard in the background – a fascinating piece of history. Joel had a great country voice and achieved minor stardom in his local area. However national stardom eluded him. He sadly passed away in 1999, aged only 51, following complications from heart surgery. Jack and Misty were listening to this CD, on which Jack is singing a whole bunch of original songs, when he heard himself singing a song he didn't remember. It was called 'Follow the Bouncin' Ball'. He said to Misty, across the breakfast table, "Hey! That's great! I sang a Roger Miller song!" Misty replied "YOU wrote that, dummy". It took him a few minutes to remember that he DID, in fact, write it, but he had completely forgotten about it.

Another time during the 1970's, Jack and Misty were scheduled to be on the Columbia/Epic show in the big auditorium in downtown Nashville. They got there early to rehearse with the orchestra and to get a feel for the stage, the lighting, and the sound. There was another act warming up on the same stage. It was David Allan Coe, who was working with a group of girl singers. When Jack and Misty walked on stage, the girls were smiling at Jack in his new black, vested tuxedo, with its rhinestone buttons and velvet lapels. David Allan Coe turned to the girls and said; "I'm going to look like that next year", and they all laughed. Misty told Jack not to let it go to his head and that it was just the tux he was wearing that had caught their eye.

In 1973 or '74, Jack and Misty were standing in line for the CMA Awards Show. They were talking to friends waiting with them. Faron Young was right in front of them and he turned, and gave Misty a big kiss and a hug. He had recently been in a car crash and Jack asked him how he was doing. Faron told them that he'd split his tongue. Jack made everyone laugh by asking, "Can you do any birdcalls?"

George Morgan was just behind them and they got talking to him. Jack had recently been to see a doctor because of recurring back pain and he'd been told the cause was kidney stones. During the conversation with George, somehow the subject was brought up. George told him not to have surgery, but to just buy a case of beer and drink one bottle after the other. The advice made sense to Jack because beer is both a diuretic and a sedative. After the awards show they went home to bed and completely forgot to buy the beer. Home at that time was their motorhome parked in The Music City Campground in LaVergne, Tennessee, a suburb of Nashville. Jack woke up in agony around 2am. He later described the pain as "a lot like giving birth to a porcupine". He asked Misty to get him to hospital and she took off for the Murfreesboro Hospital at about 60 miles an hour, with cans and dishes flying out of the cupboards and the TV antenna still up. Jack was lying on the floor in a fetal position, moaning with pain. They got to the Murfreesboro city limits, and then realized that they had no idea where the hospital was. Just then a cop pulled them over. Once they'd explained the problem, he said, "Follow me", and shot away like a bullet. Misty tried to keep up, but he must have turned off somewhere because she lost him. Somehow, they eventually found the hospital and the nurses put Jack on a cot in the emergency room. An hour or more passed, and still no doctor had come to see him. By this time Jack would have welcomed anything, even euthanasia, to relieve the pain. Misty stormed down the hall, saw a guy with a stethoscope around his neck and asked him if there was a doctor employed there. He was miffed that she didn't recognize him as a doctor, with his new stethoscope round his neck. He said these exact words, "I'm not going to give drugs to every hippie that comes in off the street". People just weren't used to Jack's style of haircut in those days. Misty assaulted him verbally for a few minutes, and then dragged him outside to look at their motorhome which had their names, and "Columbia/Epic Records", written on it. He made a couple of phone calls to verify their identity, after which his manner changed to that of a caring doctor. He quickly gave Jack a shot and some pain pills, and put him up for the rest of the night in the children's section, presumably because there were no beds available elsewhere in the hospital. Jack woke up at 7am next morning in a room with Donald Duck wallpaper, and cartoons blaring on the TV. He got up out of bed, walked out to the parking lot, and woke Misty up to go and find his clothes. She'd had a bit of wine after the ordeal and neither of them felt great. They left the Murfreesboro Hospital, vowing to never pay them.

The pain pills ran out the next evening and they got the case of beer, as George Morgan had prescribed. Jack finished twelve or so bottles and was still feeling some pain, but by that time he was past caring much. He went into the bathroom and, in the silence, Misty heard "PING!" Then she heard Jack say, "AHA!" Her response was, "Let the man who is without sin pass the first stone". The doctor who had originally diagnosed the kidney stone had told Jack that he would probably have a lot more of them. However, much to his relief, he has never had another one since then.

On another occasion, Jack and Misty were parked behind the stage at a show they were doing together with Faron Young. Faron was sitting across the kitchen table from them in their motorhome. As they talked, Faron turned to Misty and said to her, "You know, I think you're the best female singer in Nashville". She smiled, graciously accepting his compliment. A long, uncomfortable silence followed, as it became clear that Jack was waiting for his compliment. Finally, when he couldn't stand it anymore, Faron looked at Jack and said, "I can say one thing for you. Three seconds into the record you know who it is". This compliment was more than good enough for Jack and he was still bragging about it years later.

At another show, which they were doing with Waylon Jennings, Misty and Jack were on stage preparing for the performance. Misty went to give Jack a quick hug, approaching from behind. She was both shocked and embarrassed to find that she had mistaken Waylon for Jack in the dim light. From the back view Jack and Waylon looked very alike, with similar stature, style of dress and hairstyle. Waylon turned round and laughed at her mistake, saying that he'd enjoyed the hug.

During the late sixties and early seventies Jack and Misty helped run a club in Orlando. They performed there regularly when they were in town, but when they were touring they booked other artists to stand in for them. One artist who regularly worked there was

Sammi Smith, who went on to win a Grammy, for both herself and Kris Kristofferson, with his song, "Help Me Make It Through the Night". One night a guy called Norm came into the club. After overhearing a conversation about them needing a new speaker cabinet, he offered to build one free of charge. He brought in the new cabinet when he had finished it. However he seemed to think that this favor gave him exclusive rights to their undivided attention. Eventually he was barred from the club for harassing the other club patrons and he took to stalking Jack and Misty near their home. This continued until he was warned off by the police, when he thankfully disappeared from their lives.

Getting paid for gigs was often a problem, especially when working on the road. Jack and Misty always tried to get a 50% deposit with the contract, because at least then they were sure of receiving half of their fee, assuming the check didn't bounce, and it was best to get the other 50% before the start of the show, to be certain of receiving it. Some of those responsible for paying the artists have been known to change their mind about parting with their cash after the show. Sometimes they would disappear before paying up; sometimes they would get their bouncers to throw them out. At one nightclub they played at, 'The Comic Book' in Jacksonville Beach, the owners even went as far as staging a phony robbery to get out of paying them. They ran around, feigning panic, showing them the empty safe with its door wide open. They promised to meet them the next afternoon with the money, but Jack and Misty waited and called in vain.

There was also the occasion, while they were out on the road, that their manager contacted BMI, asking them to send him an advance on their royalties as they were running short of money. He requested that the check be sent to him, for him to send on to Jack and Misty, as he knew where they would be when the money arrived. Instead, he got a friend to open a new bank account using

Jack's name, and he forged Jack's signature, before paying the check into this account. It was only some months later that Jack, wondering why they hadn't had a payment for a long while, contacted BMI and discovered what had happened. The money had disappeared by then and, even though they hired a lawyer to try to track it down, the bank refused to divulge details about who had opened the phony account.

At another venue, up in the Midwest corn country, they were booked into a small county fair. As there were no dressing rooms on the fairgrounds, they were given a room in a small Mom and Pop Motel to change in. They were told to relax and that somebody would be sent to get them when the fiddle contest was over. They came twenty minutes later than the contracted starting time, saying that the fiddle contest ran overtime. The organizers then suggested that Jack and Misty take a 50% discount in their payment, seeing as they would be starting after the contracted time. However they changed their minds after the band members closed in on them, threatening that if they didn't pay 100% they might lose their teeth.

They fared better the time when they were playing at the huge Citrus Bowl in Orlando. On the show with them that day were Jerry Reed, B.J. Thomas, The Flying Wallendas (a famous high wire act, who performed without a safety net) and T.G. Sheppard. The organizers had spared no expense. There was a 35 foot high wall of speakers behind them on stage, and the sound was operated from a tower, built for the occasion, in the center of the football field. The lighting and stage crew were also first class. They were the next act on after the Wallendas, and before Jerry Reed and his band. Before the show Jack had checked out where the office was and as soon as they finished their set, while Jerry was on stage, he made a bee-line for it to get their money. A bit later T. G. Sheppard came up to them, asking if they knew where the guy with the money was. He had disappeared, having done a runner with the money. A number of years later a young man came up to them and told them it was his father who had put on that Citrus Bowl show. He said they were the only act to get paid that day. He apologized for his dad, who apparently had a habit of going underground with the payroll. He said he didn't know where the old man was and hadn't heard from him in years. They had gotten lucky that day, but there were many other occasions when they were less fortunate.

During one of their trips Jack and Misty planned to revisit Miamisburg in southern Ohio, the town where Jack had spent much of his childhood. Somehow they had missed the turnoff. They went back to where the highway should have been and found a narrow, old road with grass growing up through the cracks in the pavement. Could this really be the main road to the town that Jack remembered from his childhood? The sign said it was.

    The small city, after slumbering quietly for generations, had become a boomtown with the coming of a large chemical company. For a while, the population grew with the influx of labor. As the town opened up, the little corner taverns, where old cronies had once exchanged worldly wisdom, became juke joints. Housing became scarce, money became plentiful, and the townsfolk began a new habit of locking their doors. That was how it had been the last time he'd seen the place, the only memory he had to go by. He was surprised at the desolate, weeded-over road that had once been a main artery. They turned off the superhighway and followed the rustic lane toward the town, trying to spot familiar landmarks. There were new shabby buildings, some vacant and boarded up. There were new gas stations, looking aged and toothless, with their pumps gone. He thought he recognized an old building, a certain curve in the road, but the adjacent clutter made it impossible to get his bearings.

    As they drifted into town, he was relieved to see the railroad station and its surrounding park had been untouched by time. He had often told Misty about the good times at Aunt Bess' house, where he'd spent a lot of his childhood. Now he was about to show her the actual place where it all happened, but at first he couldn't find it. It used to be right there, on the corner of Fourth and Maple. The only thing there now was an ancient, rundown, Frankenstein-looking house hiding in the weeds. They parked while he stared at it for a long time.

Jack had somehow blocked out the memory that the whole smiling, partying family had died off one by one since he'd been gone. The small grocery store across the street had a new name, but looked the same. He went in and asked, but they didn't remember who had lived in that corner house. They didn't recognize any of the names he mentioned. Asking around he learned that the chemical plant had laid off thousands of workers, and the government had built a superhighway that bypassed the town, so it went quietly back to sleep, a little the worse for wear. They searched the town all day and it was sunset before they found anyone they knew. They were all together, as always. The squeak of the rusty wrought iron gate pierced the evening stillness as they entered the old cemetery and began brushing away weeds and dust to peer at names on tombstones, names that clicked on faces to match in his mind. They drove out of town and didn't talk for a while. Nobody said goodbye.

Early one winter, on the way to yet another gig, Jack and Misty were traveling high on the mountain curves of The Blue Ridge Parkway in the Appalachian Mountains. Suddenly both of their left rear dual-wheel tires blew out with the sound of a shotgun blast. Their big motor home lurched and swayed, and their equipment trailer threatened to pull them over the cliff edge. Jack managed, with difficulty, to get the vehicle to the shoulder of the two-lane road and they found that a broken Seven-Up bottle had ripped the tires apart. Misty and Jack were in shock, but their traveling companion, Pat Patrick, a former Green Beret, showed no emotion.

Nobody had cell phones back then and they were unable to raise any help on their CB radio. Pat calmly said, "I can fix it". He left the bus and got the tools from the trunk. Jack and Misty followed, still in a daze. Pat assessed the situation and then he slid under the crippled motor home. He asked Jack to hand him the jack, which looked small and wobbly as he pumped it up. There was a little glaze of ice on the asphalt and the jack slipped. The big motor home dropped to within a half inch of Pat's face, but he didn't blink or utter a sound. He just scraped off a patch of ice and tried again. A few minutes later he had the tires changed and they were moving down the road again. Jack turned and thanked him. Pat replied, "No problem".

Pat was regarded as a family member and he acted as their roadie, carrying their heavy equipment for them. He also played chess with Jack before a performance, to calm his pre-stage nerves. Jack never cared that Pat always won. They missed him when he eventually faded from their lives.

After leaving one of their better bookings, at a large Midwestern fair, they were looking for Millville, the town shown on their next contract. Of the three maps they had bought, two didn't show the town at all. The third map showed two Millvilles, several hundred miles apart. After making some long distance phone calls, they established which Millville they needed to be at, and found that it was the one the furthest distance away, in Pennsylvania. They set off, traveling along the Pennsylvania Turnpike, which seemed like it had the world's worst potholes. By the time they found the town, they were skidding around in a sea of mud. On arrival they learned that they were to play at the Annual Firemen's Picnic.

The stage was a pile of logs with plywood laid on top. The spotlight was a bulb hung on a pole. There was no tent or cover of any kind and, with the sky threatening rain, they agreed to do the show, only on the condition that someone was willing to stand by with tarps to throw over their instruments if the rain came. The only dressing room on offer was a room at the fire station down the road. It was dark and hot, and they had to leave the windows and door open to try and keep cool, meaning that the mosquitos soon found them.

There was a good crowd at the show, all enjoying the hot dog stands, games, a merry-go-round, and other amusements on the lawn. Jack and Misty were to do two shows. The audience made up for the earlier discomforts and, after the first show, they gathered round for autographs. They completely sold out of records, pictures, and booklets. During the interval Jack felt a drop of rain. Next moment the heavens opened. Everyone rushed to the stage to cover their equipment up, all getting in each other's way. The rain never let up and the second show was canceled. They then had to load everything back into their trailer in the rain.

Amidst all the chaos, Misty was trying, in vain, to protect the new dress she was wearing with a small plastic umbrella. To her embarrassment the dress began to shrink up right before their eyes. The long ruffled sleeves were creeping up past her elbows and her skirt, formerly a mini, was now getting ridiculously short. They made a mad dash for their car, as Misty tried to hide behind Jack. Meanwhile, back at the firehouse, the guys were already drinking beer, playing cards and counting the day's take. Jack went in and explained the situation, and all present agreed to turn their backs as Misty ran the length of the main meeting hall to the back room, where she had her other clothes. Later, they were offered a beer, which they gladly accepted. They then stood in the doorway by the fire engine, looking out into the dark, waiting for the rain to stop.

There can't be many people who have sent pedal steel guitarist, Paul Franklin, home before he played his part in recording on the session he'd been booked for, but Jack did just that. Paul had driven all the way from Nashville to Muscle Shoals, Alabama, but, when Jack heard him warming up, he decided that this wasn't the Hawaiian sound he needed that evening. Instead Jack played the part himself on his old Rickenbacher steel guitar.

One of Jack and Misty's favorite session steel players was Pete Drake. Pete was the #1 Nashville session steel player in the late 60's to mid 70's and he played on many of their early sessions. On one song, he made his guitar sound like a Hammond B-3 organ. They found him to be the most thrilling steel guy to work with. He tried seemingly impossible things – and he made them work. They became good friends and Jack learned a lot from him. It was Pete who played the steel on George Jones' recording of 'He Stopped Loving Her Today', and that big steel slide was one of the hooks that sold that record.

Other great steel players they loved to record with were Lloyd Green, who worked with them after Pete Drake died, and Weldon Myrick and Buddy Emmons, each of whom had distinct and different styles. On several of their tracks, Jack played a 1934 Rickenbacher Bakellite lap steel and a 1927 National Tri-Cone all metal Dobro. He loved those instruments, but when he got broke in Nashville he sold them to Shot Jackson for $200. He later learned that together they were worth over $100,000.

During the mid seventies Corky Tittle, a drummer who they knew from Key West, called and asked Jack if he could help his friend Eddie West get some cassettes produced. Corky and Eddie came to Orlando and, while they were there, Jack mentioned to Eddie that he and Misty needed a backing band. Eddie knew Mike Miller, who lived roughly 150 miles away in Jacksonville, FL. He phoned Mike to ask if he was willing to help out, and Jack and Misty hired him and his band by long distance.

Mike traveled down with his band to Jack and Misty's home in Orlando, parked his motor home in their front yard, and rehearsed with them for a week or so. A day or two after they'd arrived, Misty noticed that Mike's motor home was on fire. She told him, and then she rushed out with two fire extinguishers and put the fire out. The dashboard and some wiring were destroyed, but fortunately the vehicle was still movable. Mike, who had been their fan for some time, was thrilled to be invited to be their band leader and he gladly accepted the invitation. He continued in that role well into the eighties and a close friendship between them was forged, which continued during the years to come.

Around 1978, at Muscle Shoals, Alabama, Jack and Misty recorded an album, together with Vassar Clements, the famous violin virtuoso. Vassar was both a violinist and a fiddle player. Though it's the same instrument, the styles of playing are completely different, with different approaches to the music. He could play country, jazz, and all the rest. He and Misty hit it off and did some great jamming together at the recording sessions. Neither one of them had a formal music education, but had that rare kind of genius mistakenly referred to as 'by ear'. Jack said, "It's more a thing of the mind and heart than the ear, an ability to play things perfectly the first time, without written music, and to play it in a new way. Vassar and Misty never had to retake or overdub an instrumental part, getting it just right first time".

In 1979 Jack and Misty dropped out of the Country Music industry due to health problems. A couple of years later they had both fully recovered, but they'd lost their place in Nashville and their manager had died. After recording on a half dozen major labels, they were now without a recording contract. They went to work anyway, playying a wide variety of gigs, from country shows to a jazz circuit around New York State. They found some of the most ornery groups were in The Animal Circuit; The Moose, Elks, Eagles and senior clubs, and in condos, RV Parks, and similar places.

A lot of time and effort could be spent building up good

relationships with the guys who made the bookings at these venues, only for the club to vote in a new entertainment manager, so they then had to start over again. Also one complaint to the management, from just one person, could be enough to kill all hope of a return booking. Even trivial complaints could cause problems; like they were playing the 'wrong' tempo of music or that not enough people were dancing, or that the club was expecting the three musicians that they were paying for to sound like a big band. Contracts meant nothing to some of these people. Jack said that a club owner once told Count Basie, "Our crowd likes to dance at 120". The Count replied, "That's too bad. We start at nine".

One thing the Animal Circuit taught them was this: the less musicians get paid, the less respect they get.

CHAPTER 6

Down From the Heights

The 1980s brought new challenges for Jack and Misty. The whole music scene was changing. Up until then country music shows were advertised as 'Country Music Cavalcades' or 'Country Star Parades', and they featured a cross section of stars – often as many as ten major artists on a show. There was a mixture of older and younger stars, all in it together. These shows were fun and a whole lot of entertainment for the crowds.

Early on in the eighties they were told by their agent that changes were afoot. The artists with current hits would be considered 'major artists' and everybody else was classified as 'marginal' or 'minor'. The major artists and their agents were demanding all the money, with the result that the artists who didn't have current hits were not getting booked, including the pioneers and icons of the genre. The days were coming to an end when they would be able to share the stage with the likes of Merle Haggard, Charlie Pride, Boots Randolph, Jerry Reed, Roy Clark, Jerry Lee Lewis, Tom T. Hall, Don Gibson, Grampa Jones, George Jones, Tammy Wynette, Mayf Nutter, Hal Willis, Archie Campbell, Tina Turner, Jackie Gleason, Conway Twitty, Carol Channing, Skeeter Davis, Mike Douglas, Dick Clark, Waylon Jennings, Faron Young and most of the other well known names of the era.

The next few years found them struggling to get bookings. They traveled extensively around America, playing some places where their fans came to see them, and other places where nobody knew who they were, not even the club owners. They would go from a 'Jack and Misty' concert in Dayton OH to a jazz club in Schenectady NY – anywhere where they could find someone willing to book them. Their early musical experience helped them to survive. Musicians who played in the twenties through the sixties had to know the old standards, if they wanted to get bookings. These included the pop and jazz songs from about 1920 through the forties and fifties and, for those working at piano bars, they also had to know all the old sing-along songs, barbershop songs, Irish songs and other ethnic favorites. They had started their musical careers as piano players in the days before there were many good electronic keyboards. Later, during the seventies, they were very much into the new analog equipment and they found that, with a small combo and the new keyboards, they could sound more like their recordings – and do it all live. They'd also had the experience of jamming with some of the best country bands, and they'd even played jazz with Ernest Tubb's band at the E.T. Record Shop in Nashville. Having had to learn all these different styles of music was an education that came in handy now, and this versatility saved their lives when times got tough.

After being on three major labels and having had a string of songs in the charts, Jack and Misty were facing an uncertain future. No offers seemed to be forthcoming until, many months later, in 1980, they had an offer from an indie label that they had never heard of. It was called Nu-Sound, a one-man operation, with a man named Ronny Hart at the helm. Ronny was one of the good guys and, even though his label was going under, he set up a small session for them in a little studio. There were three musicians on guitar, bass, and drums and Jack and Misty with their keyboards. They got three good cuts and one demo out of that session. Those songs included 'We've Still Got Each Other', a song about their years on the road, 'Try', 'Safe Harbor' and 'I'd Rather Be a Has-been Than a Never-was'. When Ronny closed the company doors he handed Jack and Misty the masters, plus his share of the publishing, and they parted company, wishing each other good luck as they said goodbye. Nu-Sound also released recordings of 'I Will', 'Island of Love', and 'Asleep in the Saddle', which had been recorded earlier by UA (United Artists), but never released by them.

They later did a few songs for Autumn Hill, a small label which was owned by Jim Voytek, an old friend from Miami. Autumn Hill also released a few songs that had been recorded for other labels, but which had not been previously released. However Jim had an unexpected heart attack, and died before they could get the records going.

Before his death, Jim Voytek had been dating Johnny Cash's sister, Reba. Reba gave a party for the artists from Miami at a house that belonged to Johnny. This house was later to feature in the biographical film, 'Walk the Line', which was made in 2005 about Johnny Cash's life.

It was almost closing time, somewhere on the road. The piano was out of tune and they had been singing their songs to the crowd all evening. The crowd had come to hear their country songs but, near the end of the evening, Jack and Misty felt like playing something different, just for themselves for a change. When Misty started to play a jazz piano ballad, the audience loved it. The arrangement was not planned or rehearsed. Jack was playing bass and vibes on his little Yamaha keyboard and they had a drummer playing brushes. Someone captured it on a cassette recorder, though they don't remember who. Misty's first love had always been the piano, but on their recordings she was usually playing various other keyboards in the background. They didn't have any studio recordings of her playing piano so, when they found this old tape years later, they wanted their friends to hear it. Although the recording quality was not good, with it being on a thirty year old cassette tape, Jack restored it as best he could. He said it was "a music moment frozen in time".

In 1987 Misty was involved in a car crash. She was turning left at a road junction when another driver tried to jump the red light. The other car hit the passenger side of her car, causing considerable damage. Somehow she managed to hold tight to the steering wheel, which prevented the car rolling over. She also remembers her shoes popping off her feet in the impact. The police attending the scene were amazed that she had managed to keep the car upright. Fortunately she was not seriously hurt, only suffering some cracked ribs. The other driver then tried to pin the blame on Misty. Jack and Misty said that, although their car was still driveable after the crash, from then on, in their words, "it drove in the shape of a croissant".

After coming home to Orlando, from a six week engagement at an Atlantic City casino, they were ready for a little rest and recreation. However they hadn't been home long before they got a call from Bob Marcum up in McGregor, Minnesota. He wanted them to play at an outdoor celebration on the Fourth of July. They took the booking and found it great fun. They made a lot of friends there and they stayed around Minnesota for a whole year, playing virtually every club and event in the state. While they were in that area, Steve Hall and Shotgun Red were putting on a live outdoor event at Manhattan Beach, MN, and Jack and Misty were booked on the show. The stage was a flatbed truck set in the back curve of an amphitheater-shaped excavation, dug out of the side of a hill. The mud walls sopped up the sound like a blotter. However, in spite of the poor acoustics, the Minnesotan audience was enthusiastic and they had a really good day.

The snow was starting to fall as they were traveling through Illinois, or Iowa, just before Christmas one year. They were heading for yet another show and they were trying to cheer each other up by saying that they would celebrate Christmas at a later date. The Interstate Highway was just about deserted and the snow was getting heavier. They needed somewhere to pull over for the night, but everywhere seemed to be closed up. Pulling off at the next exit, the only sign of life they could see was an old barn, from which some Christmas lights were shining. It was a little store which was selling a few groceries, along with some antiques for sale in the back.

Misty negotiated with the owner a price of two dollars a night for them to hook up their electric cable. They'd been on a long, hard tour and didn't have any presents for each other, so they picked out a few gifts from things in the store. However they didn't have any way to gift wrap them. Next thing they knew, some of the store's customers offered to wrap their presents for them. When they returned with the presents, now beautifully wrapped, these friendly townsfolk brought with them some cookies and eggnog, and they had a little party with these unusual strangers.

They awoke next morning to snow-covered scenery. They said it was a perfect Christmas, but they never found out the name of the town, or which state it was in. They just called it their 'Christmas Town'.

One of the most stressful events Jack had to deal with was the time when their friends, Emma and Ronnie, tried to commit suicide. These were two of their best friends, almost like family. Musicians in their fifties, they were coming home from a job one time when they were involved in an auto accident, and injured.

During their recovery they got hooked on pain pills. These were prescription pills, not illegal drugs, but they had a doctor who was known to be liberal in his prescribing. This doctor's reputation was known for miles around and, as a result, his waiting room was always full. Emma and Ronnie went on tour, finding doctors all over the country willing to give them all the pills they wanted. They lost their home, their health, and they got old before their time. They also went into deep depression. These were good-living people who played fine music and always kept a nice home, so it was distressing for their friends to see them like this.

Then, late one night, Jack got a phone call from Ronnie. He told Jack that he and Emma were sitting in their car, in the garage, with the motor running. They'd had enough. The reason for the call was to ask Jack to explain to their kids, who were grown and had families of their own, that this was their only way out. They didn't want to be any further burden to them. They lived 70 or 80 miles from Jack and Misty's home, so there was no way Jack could get there in time to do anything. He couldn't reason with Ronnie, so instead he told him that, if he didn't get a phone call from him every ten minutes for the rest of the night, he would call 911. This made Ronnie mad. He pleaded and cursed – but it worked.

After they managed to break their drug habit they moved to Brazil, which was Emma's home country, for a number of years. Ronnie ran a farm there and Emma, who could speak six languages, worked as a teacher and interpreter. They eventually moved back to the USA, settling on the east coast of Central Florida and they continued to stay in touch with each other during the following years.

★ Names have been changed to protect their identity.

CHAPTER 7

Out of the Limelight

Valentine's Day 1991 is a date Jack and Misty won't forget in a hurry. They were playing in Jacksonville, Florida and, between shows, Misty wanted to go and buy a new blouse. They drove to the nearby 'Pic 'n' Save' store on Dunn Avenue. Jack dropped Misty off near the door and drove thirty or forty feet to the nearest parking slot. It was just getting dark.

As he was locking the car door he heard a woman scream. He had never heard Misty scream, but it sounded like it came from the area where he had dropped her off. He started to run toward the building and saw a big guy, carrying a woman's purse, running from the door area, across the front of the building. The guy was running at top speed when he saw Jack running directly at him. They crashed head on and Jack knocked him across a bunch of shopping carts. Jack spun around and landed full weight on the point of his index finger, which bent backwards, before landing on his face. People in the parking lot ran to help, and held the guy down while someone called the police. The guy had been running toward the high chain-link fence, where he was going to throw the purse to his brother, who was waiting on the other side. The brother disappeared. Meanwhile Jack, who was bleeding from the fall, was looking for his glasses. He found them, but they were broken, rendering him almost blind.

In spite of being hurt, having been knocked almost unconscious and cutting her mouth when she was knocked to the ground, Misty helped Jack into the store to seek first aid. He had hurt his leg in the melee and he could hardly walk. He was leaning on Misty as they headed for the pharmacy. The pharmacist said he couldn't help because it would be admitting his company's liability. Jack, with his injured leg, a bent finger, his glasses broken and still bleeding profusely, reached across the counter. He grabbed the pencil out of the pharmacist's pocket, pushed him aside, took some tape from a shelf and made a rough splint for his finger. The next day they went to a walk-in medical clinic, where the doctor put a splint on his finger – backwards – holding it in the bent back position.

Later, when he realized what the doctor had done, Jack turned the splint around the right way. He was on crutches for a couple of months – and the crook went to jail. Valentine's Day was never the same for them again and, since that day, Misty never carried a purse with her again if she was out alone.

In 1992 came the tragic news that Jack's son Donn had been killed in a motorcycle accident. Jack had only recently started to get to know him again, after the years they had spent apart. Donn's mother June, Jack's ex-wife, had raised him, except for a couple of years when he lived with him and Misty. June and Jack had named him Donn, but they called him Donny when he was little. Jack said he was a beautiful kid.

Donn was all grown up when they finally met again and started to get to know each other. It took a while, as they tried to figure each other out. At first Donn had resentments toward his dad, though he tried to hide them, but they both felt something needed to be resolved. It was hard to talk directly about the real issues. Jack knew that Donn had heard a lot of things about him from his mother and grandmother, and they were not all good, though Jack admitted that some things were probably true. Donn then went away for a few more years before they tried again. They found it easier to talk this time round, as they had both had time to think things over. People told them that they walked and laughed exactly alike, and they understood each other's humor. On one of his visits, they were sitting with their wives in a barbecue restaurant when they both reached for the check. Jack said, "I've never done a damn thing for you, so I'm going to do this one thing, and then THAT'S IT!" Donn replied saying: "Aw, gee, Pops. I wanted to go to college." They all broke up laughing.

That was the last time Misty and Jack saw him alive, as far as Jack could recall. He said that whole period was "sort of mixed up" in his mind. Donn had been riding his motorcycle in traffic when the car in front of him hit the brakes. Donn's bike hit the car, throwing him off, and his head hit the kerb. It was a tragedy that the helmet he was wearing proved to be of a faulty design and the bolt, which attached the visor to it, went into his brain, causing extensive damage.

When they got the news Jack and Misty rushed from Orlando to the hospital in Fort Lauderdale. Donn lay there, looking perfectly healthy, just like he was asleep. Immediately following his admission, the surgeons had operated and found massive brain damage. Three days of extensive tests followed before Donn was pronounced brain dead. Jack talked to him anyway, not really believing that Donn was never going to regain consciousness. At the end of the three days a family member gave permission for the doctors to pull the plug, and Donn died. Both Jack and Misty were devastated. A short time later there was a small funeral in northern Tennessee, where Donn had made his home with his partner, Margaret. Jack's memory of the ceremony was very hazy, and the loss of his son hit him very hard. It was a long time before life returned to normal for him.

That same year they were contacted by Jack Gale, who wanted to produce a new CD album with them. This album, titled 'Back in

Harmony', was mostly cover songs chosen from a list that Jack Gale gave them, with only two of Jack's self-penned songs included. Jack and Misty dedicated this CD to the memory of his son, Donn.

In 1995 a book was published titled 'Definitive Country: The Ultimate Encyclopedia of Country Music'. It was written and edited by Barry McCloud. In it was a section about Jack and Misty, where it was stated that they were divorced, which was simply not true. Jack and Misty discovered this book, and the error it contained, a year or two after it was published, just at the time when they were busy trying to convince everybody they weren't dead, after having been off the music scene for so long. They were furious that this misinformation about them had been published in a book that many people might use as a factual resource and, after contacting Barry about it, he apologized. The error was corrected in later editions. However the first edition of this book is still available in many libraries.

Jack and Misty had stopped touring the country by the mid eighties, partly because their motorhome was starting to feel its age, partly because they were tired of the wandering lifestyle. They settled down to life on the outskirts of the town of Sanford, a few miles north of Orlando, and were only playing the occasional gig fairly local to their home. Many of their fans hadn't heard them for so long that they had almost forgotten them. But the close of the 1990s was to mark the end of the pre-internet era for Jack & Misty.

CHAPTER 8

New Beginnings

The start of the 21st century saw new beginnings for Jack and Misty. Jack fully embraced the digital age, after receiving a wedding anniversary gift of a new computer from their friend Wayne Kelley. He quickly learned how to use it.

A year or two earlier, he and Misty had been planning to restore all the master tapes of their recordings, but they found that the tapes had deteriorated to the extent that they were un-usable. They realized that the only way to get their music into digital format, and on to CDs, was to take the music off their vinyl records. As Jack did not know how to go about this, they took some of their records to a friend in Jacksonville, Florida. Their friend converted the songs into digital format for them. Jack then remastered these raw, digital conversions of the songs, using his little 7.5 gig computer. Once remastered, these songs, plus one new song, 'Call On Me', which they had recently recorded in their own home, went onto their first ever self-produced CD, which was aptly titled 'Back from the Dead – Volume 2'. Why Volume 2? – this was Jack's humor at work as there was no Volume 1. The resulting CD album started selling well, as news about it spread.

Shortly after the release of 'Back from the Dead', Jerry Withers, a long-standing fan of their music, heard about this newly released CD. He promptly panicked, wondering how on earth he had missed

Volume 1, but of course there'd never been a Volume 1. Jerry, from the state of Washington and a keen collector of discographies, searched the internet in vain for details of their other songs. When he couldn't find any information, he created his own website in order to start his own discography of their recordings. This was in October 1999.

Around the same time, Peter Berlin, from Florida, an old friend of Jack and Misty, was browsing the internet when he came across Jerry's website. Peter had first met Jack and Misty in 1968, during the time he was working in radio at the legendary WFUN in Miami. Back then, Jack and Misty were working at the El Bolero, a Coral Gables restaurant lounge, playing 'society pop'. Peter says, "I was having dinner there with a date one evening and I was struck with the unique quality of their sound. I struck up a conversation with Jack and we became friends. I enjoyed his offbeat sense of humor and Misty was the sweetest person you could ever meet". Soon afterward Peter was called up to military service and one of the first songs he heard, after arriving in Saigon, was 'Tennessee Birdwalk'. He was delighted to learn of their success. After his discharge from the military, he returned to work as a DJ in Miami and he regularly played their songs on his radio programs. Then they lost touch for many years.

At the time when he'd found Jerry's website, Peter was building a website for a business he had purchased. It was hosted by a good friend of his, who was one of the pioneers in website construction. His friend taught Peter about ways to take advantage of distinctive web addresses, something that few people were aware of then. Peter had been trying to get back in touch with Jack and Misty, so he contacted Jerry to try and find out their contact details. Jerry gave him what sketchy details he had and, from this information, Peter found Jack's phone number. He phoned him and told him about his discovery of Jerry's site. Jack promptly phoned Jerry, who was half-asleep when he got Jack's call, as Jack had failed to take into account the time differences between their homes. As a result,

Jerry's recall of the details of that conversation are somewhat hazy.

When Jack and Misty got to see the fledgling website, they liked what Jerry was creating and, in May 2000, this website was re-launched as Jack and Misty's official website. Meanwhile, Peter was trying to help Jerry develop the website for Jack and Misty, and he was also helping Jack to learn how to do more on his computer. Peter very much wanted to do something special for them to say thanks for all the musical enjoyment they'd given to him for so long, so he kindly bought the domain name 'jackandmisty.com' and gifted it to them. Jerry has since purchased the domain name 'jackandmisty.net', which also links to their website.

Jack was soon contributing his columns, essays and news to this new website. A short biography and details of their singles, albums and CDs were added, along with photos from their archives. In addition, Jack began to send his columns to several online newsletters, notably those complied by Doug Davis on 'Country Music Classics' and Lonnie Ratliff's website, 'Nashville Showcase'. These columns were also distributed, via e-mail, to an ever growing number of fans who signed up to receive them. He also began to send their music to internet radio stations on a regular basis and, as their airplay increased, their songs began to reach new audiences. Fans of bygone years, who thought that their heroes had dropped off the planet, were finding them again, and new fans were being made from people who had never heard their music before. A look at the guest book on their website reveals messages from fans, new and old. Many of the messages contain the words "Do you remember …?" as fans of old recalled seeing or meeting them during the years they were on the road. New fans sent messages expressing their delight at their discovery of Jack and Misty's music.

They were also invited by Colonel 'Buster' Doss, who assembled the Stardust compilation CDs for distribution to radio stations, to join his 'family'. This was quite an honor.

Jack had watched his friend from Jacksonville closely, as he'd taken the old recordings and transferred them to CD, and he soon learned how to do it for himself. Soon afterwards he started remastering the rest of their back catalog.

In preparing the old vinyl records for remastering, the first stage was to wash them all with dish detergent and then let them air dry. Then they played them on his "trusty Gramophone" to find out what songs were on them. Next, they were copied onto his computer, before Jack started working on them with the array of remastering plug-ins he used. More CDs quickly followed: 'Beginnings', 'A Little Out of Sync', 'Masters of the Keyboards', 'Jack & Misty are Crazy' and 'Two Sides – One More Time' (a remastering of their 1972 album of that name).

He also started to remaster the music of other artists who wanted to make their music available on CD. He called this facility his 'Music Hospital'. Some of the artists, whose music Jack was commissioned to restore and / or remaster, included: Mayf Nutter, Joe Sun, Marvin Rainwater, Dick Shuey, Ernie Ashworth, Herman Lammers Meyer, Hal Willis, Pat Garrett, Jackie Burns, Ken Hurley, Joel Mathis, Vernon Oxford, Marty Martel, James Marvell, Shirley Frederickson, Ray Griff, Erin Hay, Don Powell, Keith Bradford, Tony Barge and Kenny Roberts.

With the numerous programs and plug-ins on his computer, he was able to make old recordings, taken from both vinyl and tape, sound as if they had just been recorded as new CD releases.

For several years, Jack had an e-mail friend called Alex Cullum, a Scottish DJ who lived in Norway, and who hosted the country music program on Boots 'n' Saddle Radio. Alex had become an ardent fan after hearing their song, 'Just One More Song Together', which was on a Stardust compilation CD that he had received for his radio program in 2001. Soon after this, Jack and Misty made contact with Marli Slater, from Ohio. Marli shared a mutual friendship with Alex, and she too was an avid fan of their music. At Marli's request, Alex wrote a lovely review of Jack and Misty's music, which she posted on her website, 'My Kind Of Country' (www.mkoc.com). In the summer of 2006, Alex had hoped to bring Jack and Misty to Norway for a festival he was helping to organize. It would have been their first ever trip outside the USA. However a combination of circumstances – the funding for the festival being pulled by the backers, and Alex's failing health – meant that this trip never came about. Although Alex and Jack had become good friends through their correspondence, they never had a chance to meet face to face. Sadly Alex died a few months later.

Another friend they made around that time was Gayle Noble, from Boulder Creek, California. In September of 1996, Gayle's daughter had started Koko's Universe, a website dedicated to Sawyer Brown, as a home-school project. On this website she started a radio station section, with a link to a page on all the radio stations she could find. She found a few other musicians on the web and was sharing this information when she found Linkin' Park, who gave her permission to link to their site, and they linked to hers. She then began looking for more folks to link to. In August of 2001, she and her mom found Jack and Misty's website and when Koko heard 'Tennessee Birdwalk', she wanted to link to them also. So they wrote to Jack and Misty to ask permission. They bought an album from them and gave Jack some tips on getting better ranking in search engines. Gayle also offered to stream Jack and Misty's music for them, so that they could send links to DJs. Back in 2001, bandwidth was still very expensive. Fortunately Gayle and Koko's website was hosted at a friend's house, so bandwidth didn't matter, as they just paid a flat rate. Over time, the friendship between them grew and many a time, if Jack was having computer problems, Gayle was able to help him solve them. She also designed many composite photos for them to use on their website and for album covers.

In 2002 Jack and Misty had a long interview with journalist Mark Harris. This gave rise to the most comprehensive biography written up until then. Sadly Mark died a few months later. This year was also a time of family bereavement for Jack and Misty when Jack's younger sister, Virginia (Ginny), died during the Easter weekend, following many years of ill-health. A few days later he wrote a very moving tribute to her in his column, which clearly showed his fondness for her.

The following year, Jack wrote about a new neighbor who had moved in near them. This new neighbor was a bear, and they still have a bear living in the vicinity of their home. Jack enjoys an evening walk, but it is a little less enjoyable now, as he has to make sure that the bear isn't around when he wants to go out. Unfortunately some of their other neighbors leave trash and foodstuff where it is accessible to the bear, which doesn't help, but just encourages him to stay.

During the year 2004, they saw both highs and lows. The biggest high was in September, when they were inducted into the New York Country Music Hall of Fame. Unfortunately they were unable to attend the ceremony, but their award was sent to their home in Florida.

The lows of that year were the series of hurricanes that hit Central Florida late that summer, with Jack and Misty's home being right in their paths. First there was Hurricane Charley, followed three weeks later in early September by Frances. This was followed by Ivan, which produced heavy rain in their area. In October, yet another hurricane, Jeanne, arrived. With the ground already waterlogged from the previous storms, flooding was extensive. Jack and Misty were evacuated three times during this period.

They'd been living in their retired Winnebago motor home and, each time they returned home, they found that it had suffered further extensive damage, the last time rendering it uninhabitable.

For a time they thought that they would be homeless again, but a kind neighbor came to their rescue with the offer of an old trailer that he'd been planning to sell. They gratefully accepted the offer and moved in a week or so later. Thankfully they were able to rescue their most valuable possessions. They had taken the precaution of wrapping all their computer equipment up in tarpaulins, along with their old records and other valuables, and they all survived unscathed. Jack kept his friends and fans updated with news whenever he was able to get internet access.

His first foray into social networking was when he joined MySpace in 2005. Later, in 2009, he joined Facebook, where he regularly posts messages, exchanging news and jokes with his friends and fans.

Early in 2005 a new chapter in their life started, when the author of this biography, Moragh Carter, first made contact with them. Shortly after getting broadband a few weeks earlier, she heard 'Tennessee Birdwalk' being played on an internet radio station. The song caught her attention and she wanted to buy it. After failing to find it on any download site, she found their website, and e-mailed Jack to ask where she could buy it. She bought their CD, 'Back from the Dead', and she fell in love with their music. There followed two years of regular e-mail correspondence, and a few phone calls, before they first met face-to-face in April 2007. They hit it off with each other straight away and soon became very close friends.

Later that year Jack and Misty were contacted by David Thrussell, the owner of OMNI records in Australia. David wanted to compile a series of albums of their songs for distribution in Australia, and later worldwide. The first album to be released was 'Life and Death (and almost everything else)'. Jack spent a lot of time remastering the songs for this album, in order to get the best possible sound out of them. Two more albums were to follow.

Later that year Jack was contacted by a guy from Holland

named Henk Den Haan. Henk had built a website for Jack and Misty and he wanted it to be their European portal. He had great ambitions for his site. Through it, he had made connections all over the world. Moragh got involved after Henk heard that she had choreographed a line dance to 'Tennessee Birdwalk', and he encouraged her to learn how to build a website of her own for line dancing fans of Jack and Misty. He hosted the resulting website on his servers and Jerry, at Jack's request, created a link to it on Jack and Misty's official website.

After a while, however, Henk's website was becoming very unwieldy. Henk wanted to do everything his own way and was unwilling to take notice of Jack's views. It eventually got to the point where, because of the way Henk was advertising their CDs, it was starting to damage their sales. Fortunately, Jack had retained ownership of the domain name, which Henk was using under license. When Henk continued to refuse to listen to him, Jack pulled the plug on his site by moving the URL away from Henk's site, to link instead with their official website run by Jerry Withers. After Henk's site went down, Moragh found a new host for her website and Jack arranged for Jerry to amend the link to it.

For most of his life Jack had been legally blind without his glasses, which he had worn since early childhood. He hated them, calling them his 'eye crutches', but he was so short-sighted that, without them, everything was just a blur. On stage, if he was not wearing glasses, he was wearing contact lenses. Then, when he started to develop cataracts, things got worse. In the spring of 2006, after seeing an eye specialist, he underwent eye surgery to remove the cataracts. At the same time new lenses, which corrected his vision, were inserted into his eyes and he could at last see clearly without his glasses. He was over the moon with the results, saying it was like "eyesight to the blind". He spent a lot of time just looking at the detail in leaves and the texture of flowers and grass. He also discovered that colors were so much brighter than he had ever realized before.

In the spring of 2007 Moragh arranged a trip to visit the USA. In addition to meeting Jack and Misty, before going on to see her sister in Boston, MA, she also planned to visit Nashville. She had a total of eighteen e-mail friends whom she hoped to meet along the way, and she succeeded in meeting all of them.

She started and finished her trip in Orlando, staying for a few nights at a hotel in Sanford, near to Jack and Misty's home. They were initially a bit wary of this stranger from the UK, who was so keen to meet them, so they met for the first time at the hotel, before going out for a meal and starting to get to know each other better.

One evening Moragh persuaded them to meet her at a nearby country music and line dance club, 'The Barn in Sanford'. Unbeknownst to them at the time, she had arranged with one of the dance teachers there to teach the dance she had choreographed to 'Tennessee Birdwalk'. The expressions on Jack and Misty's faces were a picture when they heard their song being played and they realized what Moragh had done. Though they'd known about the dance ever since she had written it, this was the first time that they had seen it being danced. Misty bravely had a go at trying to learn it, even though she is not a line dancer. Since that first meeting, Moragh has visited them at least once a year and their friendship, supplemented with regular phone calls and e-mails, continues to grow ever stronger.

Sometime during 2007 a lovely ginger cat called 'Pippin' moved in with them. He was a beautiful cat and they became really fond of him. Tragically, a year or so later, he was found dead outside their house, apparently having been poisoned.

Later that year the second OMNI compilation was released: 'Weird Scenes Inside the Birdhouse', followed in 2008 by 'Nashville Sputnik'. These CDs, particularly the first two, sold well in both

Australia and in the USA. There was talk of a possible tour in Australia, but it never came about.

In the summer of 2008 Jack had some health problems. He had been having abdominal pains for quite some time, with it being dismissed each time by his doctor as just a stomach infection. During the latter part of August that year, there was major flooding from Tropical Storm Fay, which made history by making landfall in Florida four times. Jack had been putting off visiting the doctor again about these stomach pains but, just as the rains were starting, the pains got so severe that Misty took him to the hospital emergency room.

He was kept in the hospital and, after several tests, including an MRI, he was diagnosed with gallstones. During the first surgery, the doctor removed most of the stones and Jack was fitted with a stent. There was still one more large stone remaining. However, he then developed pancreatitis, a not uncommon, but serious complication. He was allowed nothing to eat or drink for more than a week, until the condition settled.

With no access to the internet, Jack was worried about not being able to answer the many e-mails he received daily from his fans. As Misty could not use a computer at the time, Moragh agreed to act as his internet contact while he was in hospital. She already had the e-mail addresses of some of his key contacts, like newsletter owners, and she sent messages about his hospital admission and his progress to them, asking them to spread the word. She kept in phone contact with Jack and Misty for updates on his progress, and she passed messages to and from other people back to Jack.

As he had gone into hospital just as the rains were starting, Jack did not see the full extent of the flooding. Misty, meanwhile, was literally wading, shin deep in water, to cross the hospital parking lot in order to visit him. By the time he was allowed home, the water was beginning to recede. Fortunately, in spite of Misty's fears, no water got into their home, even though it was close at one point.

Jack came home to recuperate from his surgery and the pancreatitis. He was re-admitted to the hospital a few weeks later to have the other gallstone and the stent removed. Then the following day, his gall bladder was removed. He went on to make a full recovery.

Earlier in August 2008, Misty was delighted to be able to get a new keyboard to replace her twenty-five year old favorite, for which she could no longer get replacement parts. Then in October 2009 Jack bought himself a new guitar, with the idea of using it to help him get back into songwriting again.

Then, in the spring of 2009, they had the chance to move into a new and larger home. A near neighbor needed to downsize in order to release money for his medical bills. They agreed a part exchange for a modest price and they moved into their new home in March that year. Here they had room to leave their keyboards up, instead of having to pack them away after every use. They also had a car port to protect their car from the weather. Unfortunately the old air conditioner that came with their new home broke down a few months later. They suffered five days in the sweltering heat of summer before they could get it replaced. On top of that their car had ongoing problems.

In April 2010, both Jack and Misty were notified that their driving licenses were due for renewal in May, their birth month. However the renewal process wasn't straight forward, like it had been on previous occasions. Florida had decided to implement new security rules, which meant that every applicant had to verify their identity afresh. In addition to the old driver's license, the licensing bureau wanted to see a birth certificate, marriage license, divorce papers (if relevant), two proofs of residence and a copy of medical records with the applicant's name and birth date on them.

Misty went with Jack to renew her license at the same time. She had to prove that her last name was now Blanchard, even though they had been married for nearly forty-seven years. She also had to change the spelling of her first name from Maryanne to Mary Ann on her license, to match that on her birth certificate.

When Jack got to the counter, the clerk noticed that his driver's license and Social Security card both said 'Jack Blanchard', but that his birth certificate said 'John Blanchard'. This discrepancy had never been questioned before by any of the authorities. Unfortunately, when Jack had had his surname legally changed to Blanchard, years earlier, he never thought to check that the lawyer had also changed his birth name from John to Jack, the name that he had been known by all his life.

They were told to go to the social security office in Orlando. It was a very hot, eighty-mile round trip, due to the fact that the air conditioner in their car was not working properly. After a long, uncomfortable wait at the office, Misty's identity was confirmed. Jack faced a problem though. He was told he had two choices. The clerk said to him, "You will have to change all your legal things to John … titles to your home and vehicles, your credit, your will, your bills, and everything else". The alternative option, she suggested, was that it would be easier to legally change his first name to 'Jack'. He chose the latter option, even though it cost him about $1200 in legal and other fees. They would not renew his license until he had all this sorted out, leaving him unable to drive for a whole month. He was mighty relieved when he finally received his new license, and though he was not very happy with the photo on it, his sister Valerie said it was the best driver's license picture she'd ever seen.

For her birthday that year Misty was given a laptop computer. She had wanted to learn how to use one for some time, but had never dared touch Jack's computer for fear of messing up any of his music programs. She quickly learnt the basics of how to send e-mails and photos. It also meant that they now had a computer that they could take with them when they were traveling away from home. Misty also had her own trip to the Emergency Room that summer, for a serious spider bite. The staff there were friendly and treated her well, and she quickly recovered from the ordeal.

Later that summer they re-established contact with Jack Gale, the producer of their album, 'Back in Harmony', after having lost contact with him for nearly twenty years. A month or two later they were invited to visit him at his home in Sebring, FL. They had some trepidation about visiting this town again as they'd had some bad experiences there several years earlier.

On that earlier occasion they'd secured a four-week contract at a hotel restaurant and lounge in the town, with a house to stay in as part of the deal. A major hurricane was heading toward Central Florida at the time. The hotel audiences loved them, but the management hated them, and they couldn't understand why. They noticed whispering among the staff, which was not a good sign. By the first weekend the management was openly hostile. Then the owner yelled at them, in front of the crowd, saying that they should have known better than to sing their song, 'Cows', in a steak house. That Sunday night, just as the hurricane was beginning, there was a knock on their house door. They were told that they were fired and their contract was not going to be honored. They were given twelve hours to move out, along with all their heavy equipment. The owner told their agent that they'd used improper material, threatening to ruin his business.

They'd always felt that there was more to this episode than they knew at the time and, shortly before the trip to Buffalo in the fall of 2010, they believed that they might have finally solved the mystery. They were sitting in their living room, talking about how hard it had been to quit smoking. Misty had been going cold turkey at the time and Jack was "burning his tongue" with a pipe. Misty mentioned that, during that terrible week in Sebring, she'd had no cigarettes in the house so, whenever Jack went into town, she'd get some of his pipe tobacco, roll it up in a paper towel, and try to smoke it. The result of her efforts looked like gigantic marijuana joints and she would go out into the backyard to smoke them, so as not to set the house on fire. They looked at each other, as the realization dawned on them, and said, almost in unison, "That must be why they got rid of us!" The neighbors must have seen Misty and thought that she was smoking enormous amounts of dope on a daily basis, and complained to the hotel owner.

However this latest trip to Sebring, to visit Jack Gale, was completely different. They had a very pleasant afternoon talking with him and his wife Lovey, after which they were treated to a very nice meal at Jack and Lovey's favorite restaurant.

A few weeks earlier, they had received the news that they had been nominated, by a DJ friend, for induction into the Buffalo (NY) Music Hall of Fame. Not long after, they heard that their nomination had been successful, and they were invited to attend the ceremony. As they'd always hated flying, Moragh agreed to share the driving to Buffalo. The ceremony took place on October 7th 2010. They had a marvelous time during this trip and, because they were traveling by road, they were able to visit family and friends en route, people who they rarely got to see. It was a double celebration that evening, as October 7th was also their wedding anniversary.

Before going to Buffalo, Jack made a new compilation CD, 'Traveling Music', which he sent to CD Baby (www.cdbaby.com/cd/jackmisty). He also made a sampler CD, with one minute samples of 26 of their songs, for free distribution to people they met in Buffalo, and to others who showed an interest in their music.

Over a late-morning coffee one day, Jack and Misty were reminiscing when Jack asked Misty this question. "All in all, what do you think were the best places we've stayed, like apartments, houses, motels, and so on?" She replied, "That's easy," and named three. They were 'The Sea Palm' at Saint Simon's Island, off the coast of Brunswick, Georgia, which had provided the best accommodation, 'Key Colony Beach', a place called a 'boatel' – like a motel for boats, which was situated between Key Largo and Marathon, Florida, and a lodge on top of a high mountain at Lake Arrowhead, California.

Saint Simon's Island sits in the blue Atlantic Ocean. The job came with a luxury apartment overlooking a small river. Tropical flowers, trees and shrubs were trimmed neatly and the riverside grass was like a putting green. Misty liked to sit on the grass and watch the ducks. One particular duck liked to sit with her. It moseyed up to her one afternoon, quacked a few pleasantries, sat by her, tucked in its feet, puffed up a little and stayed there for as long as Misty stayed. The job was for just the two of them. They had all their keyboards, and sounded like a big band, with nothing pre-recorded. Nobody knew who owned the place and the rumor went around that Jack and Misty did. The lounge manager asked Jack if it was true, but he just said, "Shhh, I can't talk about it". They became the royal hosts of a month-long wild party, and got paid for it.

At 'Key Colony Beach' the apartments were built on pilings, like a long pier. Jack and Misty had the last apartment, way out in the ocean. Porpoises played outside the big windows and, when the tourist fishing boats came in at sunset, hoards of seagulls and pelicans would gather noisily, vying for the leftover fish that was tossed overboard. They had their five piece band in the restaurant / lounge, at the entrance of which was a huge, decorative champagne glass that bubbled as long as it was plugged in. Nobody in their band drank, so when customers bought them cocktails they would dump them in the fake champagne glass. They hadn't realized that the water was being continually recirculated, but soon they could see swirling orange peel, olives and other garbage, and the imitation champagne had taken on a peculiar color. When they realized their mistake they tried to look innocent. Fortunately the owner was a nice guy and he never brought it up. When they'd arrived the Steinway grand piano was still upside down, the way Hurricane Donna had left it in 1960. When a bunch of guys turned it right side up for Misty, it played beautifully. Their drummer, Roy, had made friends with the chef and, one evening, he smuggled out a couple of live lobsters to take to his apartment. In a hurry, he tied them onto the bumper of his car, which was parked in a dark place, but they either escaped or were stolen. He was not pleased to find them gone.

The lodge at Lake Arrowhead, California was on top of a high mountain. It was a summer night when they checked in, but the next morning, when they pulled the cord on the drapes that covered a whole wall-sized picture window, they saw that the mountain forest outside was covered in two feet of new snow, without a sign of life except for some rabbit tracks by their window. They said it was the most beautiful, real-life, Christmas card they had ever seen – and this was in California, in June.

In May 2012, their old friend and ex-band leader, Mike Miller, arranged a recording session for them at Ozone Studios in Jacksonville, Florida, to record a new CD. Most of the songs for this session, which were all written by Jack, had been recorded by other artists, but never recorded by Jack and Misty. Jack was also beginning to break through a long-standing writer's block and starting to compose new songs again, but none of these were ready for recording at this session.

Earlier in the year they'd been invited back to Buffalo for the Music Hall of Fame's 30th anniversary on October 4th 2012. Moragh flew to join them to share the driving with them again. As this book had not yet gone to press she brought some flyers with her which were distributed along the way. Many more stories were recalled during this trip, but these will have to wait for the sequel which, provided she lives long enough, Moragh hopes to write.

CHAPTER 9

Jack's Stories
– a short selection

A few of Jack's stories are included, as written by him, to give you a taste of his serious and humorous writings. They are included with his permission.

★ ★ ★ ★ ★

"Today I Went Outside"

Today I went outside and was surprised to find the real world. The sky was exactly the color of my monitor screen, the sound of the birds was in remarkable stereo, and the dogs, cats, and people were cleverly animated. There were no pop-ups, unless you count the butterflies, and they carried no advertising. The entire display was completely wireless, which was fortunate, because I could find no wall plugs on the horizon.

There was an odd sort of email. It was made of paper, and delivered by a grown man in shorts. I was amazed to find that I could chat with friends without typing!

I sat on the front steps of my home page, opened my brown bag, and enjoyed a lunch of Spam and cookies. After several hours it all became dark, so I assumed that it had crashed, and tried to restart it. I gave up after waiting almost all night. Although the real world is quite slow, and probably an obsolete version, I plan to go outside and attempt to reboot it again some time.

★ ★ ★ ★ ★

Liner notes on Tom T. Hall's album (as written by Jack at Tom's request)

WARNING:
DO NOT hold this album under the hot water faucet, because the people living inside the record might pop out into living 3-D, right there in your kitchen … or even worse, your bathroom. The crowd might be hard to explain to the landlord.

This same warning applies to any Tom T. Hall record because of his secret recipe for canning real people like you and me and Luther Short into plastic discs, without losing the original flavor.

The characters in his songs act completely on their own, sticking up their noses at Mr. Hall. They couldn't care less if he is stuck without a romantic ending, or an earthshaking moral. They've got their own troubles, and they work them out in their own way. Thanks to the miracles of science, we can eavesdrop in living stereo.

Heroes and beautiful people are the usual favorites of storytellers, but Tom T. finds poetry in us ordinary hairy-legged mortals, with our petty selfishness, hypocrisy, and intolerance … our weaknesses, and our occasional goodness.

So, step inside. You're likely to run into yourself somewhere in this record.

And, oh yeah, as I said at the beginning ... Keep this record dry, and out of the reach of children. And please keep Tom T. Hall's picture off the floor if you have pets.

★ ★ ★ ★ ★

THE SUNSET TRAIN

Prologue:
[This story is not new. It was originally a song Jack wrote back in the sixties. They liked the song, but song lyrics have limitations. They are necessarily 'bare bones', so he wrote the story to fill in the details. It was based partially on reality: Misty and he actually had the painting. The 'real' one was titled: 'The Red Caboose', painted by Paul Detlefsen. They had just bought a tract house in Miami with no down payment, and had no money for furniture or curtains for the windows. Jack said the painting was waiting for them at the 'W.T. Grant' store. It was big, beautiful, and under $20. They lost the house, and moved a lot, but they always kept the picture. It represented home.]

The Story:
He headed for the cashier's counter, hoping that the curtain rods he was carrying were the ones she wanted, when he saw it for the first time. Funny! He'd been in this store, and up and down these aisles dozens of times, but he had never noticed those wall pictures before. He wasn't much of an art critic, he guessed. Didn't really know much about it, but he DID know he'd never seen anything quite like that train picture.

The surface of the picture was textured to look like a genuine oil painting, and somehow that scene looked MORE REAL THAN LIFE! The silver steam from the old engine glowing in the sunset, billowing against the yellow-blue-orange-pink sky. The brightly colored, but weather worn railroad cars. The red caboose so real you could almost step right into it. Each piece of gravel along the track, each clump of vegetation on the lonesome prairie clearly defined and casting a long, late afternoon shadow. The mountains were a bluish haze against the distant horizon. It was a painting you could stare at for a long time, finding details previously overlooked.

A bell rang. The store was closing. On impulse he hurried to the Customer Service Desk and put the picture on 'layaway' with five dollars that should really have gone toward overdue bills. He didn't know when he'd be able to manage the eleven-ninety-five balance. He paid for the curtain rods and went home, feeling a little guilty.

She stood back and looked critically at the curtains she'd hung. He told her that they sure made a big difference in the little apartment. She laughed that, at least, the curtains looked better than the view of the trash cans in the alley. He held her and said he wished he could provide her with a decent home, with enough furnishings to go around, and she replied that they weren't doing too badly for newlyweds, and that she believed in him. He didn't mention the money he'd foolishly spent on a picture of a train.

Pay day again, and another losing battle with arithmetic. If only a single tree or a patch of grass could be seen from their window, it might raise their spirits by interrupting the stark drabness surrounding their dingy apartment. He felt especially sorry for her, being stuck there all day. At least taking the bus to the factory everyday gave him a change of scene. These were his thoughts as he paid the cashier and waited for the large picture to be wrapped.

He centered it carefully on the wall over the big easy chair with the broken spring, and called her to come in from the kitchenette and take a look at the 'surprise'. Wiping her hands on her apron, she glanced around the room until her eyes stopped at the unexpected explosion of color. It was so beautiful she almost cried! Why, it was just like having a window overlooking a lovely peaceful valley locked in eternal sunset. They held hands and stared at the painting until dinner almost burned.

Years struggled by and the broken spring chair was replaced by a new living room suite, complete with payment book. They moved several times in the course of their lives, first to a couple of larger apartments, then to a house in a suburban development and finally, anticlimactically, back to another cheap apartment where they were to spend their autumn years.

The infirmities of old age often require a tightening of purse strings. They weren't complaining though. They'd been through rough times before. Through the years they'd managed to hang on to two treasures: The Sunset Train painting and an undying love for each other. Perhaps they weren't so poor after all.

It hit him hard when she passed away. Somehow, he'd always imagined he'd be the first to go. He wasn't prepared for the horrible emptiness. Nobody ever is. He took the habit of conversing with her, even though she was gone. He'd stare at the painting and talk over old times. Sometimes he'd sit for hours in front of the television, but his eyes would wander back to the Sunset Train, their most prized possession. He'd imagine that they were together in that valley, or riding on the train itself. The neighbors, aware of his condition since her death, occasionally dropped in to check on him. Conversations always gravitated to the unusual picture.

Several days had passed before anyone noticed the newspapers accumulated outside his front door. Fearing the old man had died and, after receiving no answer to their knocking and calling, the neighbors set their shoulders to the door, and the old wood gave way. Finding no one in the apartment, all clothes intact in the closets, and the television left on, the neighbors notified the police of the old man's disappearance. They arrived shortly after.

While the premises were being inspected, an officer casually commented to a neighbor, "Unusual painting in there! So realistic, I mean". "Yeah," replied the other, "everybody remarks about that train picture. It's real pretty." "No," said the policeman, "I'm talkin' about that big picture of the valley and the sunset. There's a railroad track runnin' through it, I guess, but no train. Yep, I'm absolutely sure there was no train in that picture."

And that was absolutely right.

Epilogue:
They had first bought the big picture in a discount store and had it in their first house. Jack had written a story and a song about that picture. After the excitement of hit records, and when the money and fame had faded, they found themselves, almost twenty years later, going through a rough bankruptcy. Their big homes, sports cars, and belongings were being sold off. They salvaged a few things and moved into a trailer park. The Sunset Train painting was left with a friend, along with some other memorabilia, for safe keeping, until they could get settled somewhere. More years flew by, and the friend began to think their stuff was hers. They never got it back, and couldn't find a replacement, so all they had left of the old train was a sketch Jack drew as a promotion for the record.

This song was among their very first Nashville recordings, and the only copy they had was an old 45 in terrible condition. They cleaned it up the best they could, and it found a place on their 2005 CD 'Life and Death' on Omni Records ... a major Australian label. Jack put the story in his column which was sent out to fans, as well as being posted on his website.

One day a great big package arrived containing a painting of 'The Sunset Train'. It came from an anonymous benefactor. They had no idea who sent it, but they were grateful to have it back in their lives.

One of the first things they did when they moved into their new place (in 2009) was to hang the painting of the 'Sunset Train' in a place of honor. It's not an original painting ... just a print, but it has been in their life since Misty and Jack started out together, and it had become a member of the family.

★ ★ ★ ★ ★

HENHOUSE MURDER TRIAL BEGINS.
Reporter: Jack Blanchard

Jury selection has begun in the notorious Henhouse Murder trial of Adrian "Cluck" Rydzinek, suspended county livestock inspector accused of the killing of seven hundred thirty-one chickens, three pigs, one horse, and the assault of Mrs. Fanny G. Heimeier, 87, of Heimeier Farms, Inc., 8212 Wyless Road, who had been sitting innocently on the porch.

Herman Heimeier, the farm owner, according to police reports, returned from a delivery to find his farm a bloody mess, and the assault of his grandmother already in progress. According to Heimeier, she shouted, "Keep out of this, Herman. I can handle it!" Mr. Heimeier, nevertheless, clubbed Rydzinek into submission with a deceased chicken.

Judge Fearn B. Fowler, in a preliminary hearing, ruled that the charges would be "Destruction of property, because chickens are not people, and not subject to murder", and the assault charge would hinge on the statements and attitude of Mrs. Heimeier, who has not spoken since the incident. Doctors are encouraged by the pleasant smile that never leaves her face.

Court appointed Psychiatrists believe Rydzinek was suffering from "Chicken Fatigue". After twenty-six years of chicken inspecting he just snapped. "Suddenly I hated every chicken in the world", sobbed Rydzinek, when taken into custody. He made no mention of the pigs, the horse, and the grandmother.

[Jack said: "The Henhouse Murder was run as a real news item. The proofreader at the paper thought it was news, and not one of my columns. He left out my picture and byline. Caused quite a stir in Orlando. We came into our club that night and heard people at the bar talking about the county inspector who went berserk. That's funnier than the story."]

★ ★ ★ ★ ★

"The One And Only Eddie Simmons"

When I first got to Miami I answered some help-wanted ads for piano players. One was at The Sportsman's Lodge, a restaurant and lounge which sat right in the driveway of The Hollywood Dog Track.

I auditioned for a man in his fifties named Eddie Simmons. I thought he was the owner, because he had an air of authority. He was small, wiry, and bald, except for a fringe of dark hair. His nose pointed straight out like Pinocchio or Cyrano, but his Sean Connery eyes nailed you to the wall. There was also a little of the sad clown about him.

It turned out that Eddie was the singer and drummer who would work as a duo with me. He had one of the greatest voices I've ever heard ... the depth of Barry White, with Al Jolson's power. He didn't need a mike. When Eddy sang, he was an actor drawing the crowd right in. Everything Eddie Simmons did he did with a flair. He'd come out from behind the drums, during a song and sing personally to women in the crowd. It would have been corny if I had done it, but Eddie had the touch.

One week the chef was out sick and Eddie cooked for the whole place, making it look easy. I saw him take a head of lettuce out of cold water, and slam it down on the counter. The core dropped right out and the lettuce opened like a flower. He'd switch from the chef's apron and hat to a waiter's jacket, and glide out from the kitchen with heavy laden trays of food held high over his head, and serve it with a flourish, a smile, and a bow ... like a magician.

Eddie had problems, but he didn't let the public know it. One was alcohol and the other: women. He married a nice lady named Betty who got pregnant and stayed that way for about ten months. The last few months she looked like the Queen Mary. A doctor finally told her it was a "false pregnancy", and she immediately deflated. It was all in her mind. She left Eddie for a Norwegian sea captain.

Eddie did what alcoholics do, but his singing was still genius, especially the blues. The last I saw of Eddie he was going with a lady alcoholic. It was sad to see them drinking their lives away. Eddie Simmons was a star the world lost before he was found. I wish you could have heard him sing 'When It's Sleepy Time Down South'.

IN HARMONY

★ ★ ★ ★ ★

PLEASE HELP OUR WILDLIFE.

It's a cold winter, and hard on our wildlife.
We feel it's our humane and patriotic duty to provide warm headgear for our American Bald Eagles.

A $10 tax exempt donation will provide a plaid hunting cap with earflaps for a cold bird.

A $50 donation will supply a stylish toupee for some lucky fowl, and you will receive a color photograph of YOUR eagle wearing it.

Please send your donations to:
W.H.A.T.F.E.B.B. (Warm Hats And Toupees For Every Bald Bird)
Lake Monroe, Florida

Thank you.

Jack Blanchard, Chairman.

★ ★ ★ ★ ★

"The Last Day"

Simon Lescart woke up on his last day, plugged in the coffee maker, and sat down at the computer to check his email. There was the usual spam and forwarded jokes, which he deleted without reading. The sixth message subject line read "Final Notice", and the sender was an acronym "T.P.T.B." He started to dump it as spam, but for some reason he clicked it open.

The message was this: "NOTICE OF EXPIRATION.

"Dear Mr. Lescart, This is an automatic reminder that your life expires at midnight tonight. Please do not try to reply to this email. Have a nice day.
Very truly yours,
The Powers That Be."

Simon tried to reply anyway, but his email bounced back from the unknown recipient. He knew it was most likely a stupid joke, but he couldn't stop thinking about it as he fought the city traffic on his way to work.

What if this really was his last day? He'd often heard the old saying, You should live every day as if it were your last. What should a person do on his last day, anyway? Get drunk? Smell some flowers? Confess his sins? What?

He didn't have much of a family to visit, just a brother up in Akron, and an ex-wife in Atlanta. They hadn't spoken in years. He couldn't think of any old sins offhand. Maybe he should commit some? He knew that the weird email was a fraud, but he decided not to go to work today, just in case. He pulled off at an exit, and got back on the expressway going the other way toward the ocean. This is nuts, he thought. He couldn't think of anything really important to do, befitting a person's last day on the planet, so he just sat on the beach for most of the day, and drank a few beers. He felt a little nervous, like a high school truant, but he also felt something else he couldn't define. Was it freedom? He had some guilt too, for wasting the day looking at the ocean.

Someone, whose approach he hadn't noticed, sat down beside him.

The man was obviously homeless, in his ragged black suit and dirty torn sneakers. The man said, "Are you okay, friend? You look kinda lost".

   Simon said this: "That's an odd word 'Friend'. Now that you mention it, I guess I don't have any of those, just a bunch of acquaintances". "Maybe you never really tried", said the man. "I've been pretty busy", said Simon. "You must have accomplished a lot of great things being so busy", the man said. "No great things. Just keeping even. Paying the bills", said Simon. "Do you think you have any great things in you?" asked the man. Simon said, "Maybe. I've been doing a lot of thinking. If I had the time I'd do things differently."

That's when the chest pain struck, and the world faded to black. He vaguely heard voices "What Happened?" "Get back!" He was being carried. Then a blinding light above. People working over him. "We're losing him!" "Clear!" Then a huge shock. The world was gone again.

The smiling nurse said, "Welcome back. You've had quite a day." "What time is it?" he asked. "Almost midnight", she said. "I have to call my brother", he insisted. "We'll contact him for you. You can talk to him in a few days." "I wish I HAD a few days!" he said.

A cell phone rang. "That sounds like mine", he said. "Where is it?" "It's beside your bed, but you need to rest." He tried to reach for it, but she stopped him. "I'll answer it for you", she said. "Lie back down!" She said, "It's just a text message". "What does it say?" he gasped. The letters on the cell phone screen said this: "EXTENSION GRANTED."

★ ★ ★ ★ ★

"Somewhere in Colorado"

We were playing at a fair. The grandstand was about a hundred years old, with aged, weathered wood and no paint. An hour before show time a small airplane landed in the field beside the stage. The door opened and Hank Thompson got out in his white suit and white hat. We thought that was pretty cool. Hank was the other half of our bill that day.

Misty had six electronic keyboards stacked up in a horseshoe shape around her onstage. Then the rest of our band and all the amps and sound equipment. It took some electricity. This stuff wouldn't work if the voltage was low, so I had our tech guy build a thing he called a Variac. The Variac told you if you were getting low voltage, and you could just turn it up until you got the volts you wanted.

The fair people had run a long yellow drop cord from the grandstand out to the stage, and it looked pretty thin to me. I saw we were only getting about 98 volts, so I cranked the Variac up to 117, and everything worked. What a great invention!

About three songs into our show our steel player tapped me on the shoulder and pointed down at the yellow wire. Flames were running along it like the fuse to a bomb, along the grass and right up the wooden pillars of the old structure. The fire department came and hosed down the whole show.

★ ★ ★ ★ ★

"The Tear"

There's something about a photograph. Many people believe that having your picture taken steals some of your soul. I look at pictures of friends and relatives who have died, and I can see that soul, especially in the eyes, the expression, and even the body english.

I have a picture of my mother taken at a holiday gathering during her later years. She was smiling, and seemed to be in the Christmas spirit. I've looked at that picture many times, but a few weeks ago, I enlarged it, and thought I saw something.

I hit the 200% button, made it really big, and zoomed in on her face. The smile was still there, but in her eye I saw something unexpected: A tear.

I sat back in shock and took a deep breath. What could she have been thinking? Was it a tear of joy or sadness? Did she know that it may be one of her last family moments? I asked her that question aloud, but the photograph didn't answer.

I'm sure we were all enjoying the moment together, but at the same time, taking it for granted. You always think there will be many more. Now I realize my mother was not taking that moment for granted.

I keep going back to look at the photo, even though it's burned into my mind, and my heart. When I discovered the tear behind her smile, I had tears to match hers. We spoke to each other beyond the limits of time and space. There is soul in a photograph.

★ ★ ★ ★ ★

CHAPTER 10

Further Insights

Jack has written several hundred stories and columns, most of which can be found on his website. Many of these stories reveal various facets of his character, along with snippets about his relationship with Misty. He has written about things that they love and hate; their struggles and joys; their adventures on the road and in the music business; his opinions on matters great and small. Some stories are serious, some humorous and several are pure fantasy. Further insights about them have been gleaned from conversations, both face-to-face and via e-mail.

Many of his stories are based on truth, but the story has been expanded and embellished, and readers need to get to know him well before they can extract truth from fiction with any certainty. Other stories are so obviously fiction that there is normally no problem. However there was one notable occasion when a newspaper reporter failed to recognize that a story about a chicken inspector going on a killing spree was a spoof, and he caused quite a stir when the story was reported as fact in the local newspaper. Many other stories were written just to give his readers a good laugh.

He loves to write about Misty, making it clear how much he still adores her. He says frequently that they are both friends and lovers, with the things that they have been through together bringing them closer, and they never are at a loss for something to talk about.

Although they both had children from their first marriages, they never had a child from their relationship together, but he has written, "Love and friendship are good, each by itself, but to find them both together is a bonus blessing. I am lucky. My wife is my best friend, and the nicest human I know. Anybody who doesn't like her probably has a mean streak. Misty often inspires me to write songs about friends in love".

He also says, "Misty has a photographic memory for music. She can play any piece she hears once, even if it's just background Muzak in a store, but she does not read music. She has never sung a single note off key. She can play all kinds of music, and her ear for sound is a valuable tool I use when mixing sessions. I can write the songs, and we work out the arrangements together, but she has the final word on the mixdowns. When I write a new song I sing it to her first. She never says it's bad. If she says, "That's really nice", I know it isn't. I have to go back and work on the song until she gives the right reaction. It's sort of an excitement in her eyes … sometimes even tears. She's always right. My final editor.

"She is the perfect straight man to my funny stuff. She folds her arms and gives me a look that says this: "Whenever you're through, dummy. We're trying to do a serious show here". The audiences love her, and so do I."

Apart from their love for each other, the one thing that stands out is their love for their dogs. In fact they refer to them as their children and they have owned several during their years together. The first was Brubeck, named after their favorite jazz pianist, Dave Brubeck. Brubeck looked like a Jack Russell Terrier, but wasn't. People would often remark about his good looks and when they asked what breed he was Jack would tell them that he was a miniature Armenian Shepherd, a breed he had made up. This was easier than trying to explain Brubeck's mixed ancestry. Jack said that he was a wonderful dog, an intelligent and faithful friend to them. His one fault was that he was a fussy eater, refusing dog food in favor of cat food or the special concoctions that Misty would cook for him. But he would happily eat motel mattresses, linoleum floors, and Jack's better clothes. They were living in Miami at the time when they came home one day, after doing a live radio broadcast, to discover that he had been killed by a car. They were devastated.

A few months later they bought a bassett hound puppy called Cecil. When they moved to Key West, Cecil went with them. However he proved impossible to train and he bit anyone he could get his teeth into. When they went to work they would lock him in the bathroom, which he destroyed. They noticed something wrong with his throat and the vet told them that he had damaged it by howling all night while they were at work. They couldn't keep him and, after asking around, the Mayor of Key West agreed to take him. A woman, possibly the Mayor's wife or his assistant, came to pick him up and he went happily with her without looking back. They never knew how they fared in his new home.

Misty came home one day with a whippet, a miniature greyhound, named Prince. He was very thin and shaky and they wondered if he had been abused. He was very insecure, but a sweetheart, and they let him sleep between them. When they had to go away for a week they entrusted him with neighbors. When they returned they found him hiding under the neighbors' trailer, with bad burns from hot liquid. Misty grabbed him and took him home but, much as they loved him, they knew they couldn't keep him. They knew a very nice young woman who was thrilled to take him. Sadly Prince was killed by a car as she was walking him across a street on a leash.

They were on a tour arranged by The ABC Talent Agency, traveling throughout the Eastern states, and they were in Montgomery, Alabama, when they got their next dog. He was a toy poodle whom Jack described as "a puffy silver beauty", loved by everybody. They named him Wolf, short for Wolfgang Amadeus

Mozart Blanchard. Wolf was very smart and quite a comic. In fact, Jack said that if a dog could be a genius, then Wolf fitted the bill. He knew a lot of tricks and also knew how to manipulate people. When he wanted to go out he would fetch his leash and carry it to Jack or Misty. When Misty was trying to teach him to fetch, Wolf would nudge the toy off the seat with his nose, and then look up at her for help. Misty would reach down to the floor and put the toy back up on the seat. Wolf would wait a few minutes and then knock it off again. Jack watched for a while and then realized that Wolf had taught Misty to fetch. Jack had also noticed that his socks were disappearing and, one day, they saw one slowly being pulled under the bed, where Wolf was hoarding them. Wolf liked getting under the bed and sometimes he refused to come out. Eventually they worked out a way to entice him out. Jack would go outside and ring the doorbell and Misty would yell, "Who is it?" Wolf would then tear out from under the bed, barking all the way to the door, and they would grab him. Smart as he was, he fell for it every time.

He looked to be an exceptionally healthy dog, but then he began to have some seizures. These were frightening to watch, but they didn't realize at the time that Wolf was diabetic. They were about to go on a brief tour, so while they were gone they boarded him at a highly rated boarding kennel in Orlando. After not hearing any news for several days, they called to ask how he was doing. The receptionist went to enquire and came back with the message, saying, "Oh, that dog? It died". They were deeply shocked and saddened by this loss. They were later told his death was due to pancreatic failure.

A while later they went to a Winter Park pet store, to find a replacement for Wolf. There, in a cage, they saw another toy poodle. As soon as he was let out he made a beeline for Misty and seemed to run right up her, into her arms. It was love at first sight. They named him Wolf 2. He was a complete contrast in personality to Wolf 1. He took life very seriously, always trying to be on his best behavior. Shortly afterwards Misty brought home a blonde Lhasa Apso puppy with huge eyes and fur sprouts like a porcupine. "Her coat will get long and beautiful", Misty said. They named her Camille, after the old Garbo movie. Wolf and Camille loved each other's company and, as they got older, Wolf would take care of Camille, even when she was old and blind, guiding her around the house. Wolf and Camille lived together for about sixteen years.

They were living in Nashville when Wolf developed a spinal problem, causing him to suddenly lose the use of his hind legs. People who saw Misty carrying him around told them they should have him put down, but they refused. Money was short but, after making some enquiries, they found a surgeon willing to operate on him free of charge. For several months following the surgery Wolf needed to be regularly catheterized by Misty, and he was struggling to walk. Then one day Misty came in, laughing and happy, shouting. "He just peed on his own!" They were overjoyed with his progress and he eventually learnt to run perfectly, even though he continued to walk with some stiffness in his hind legs. When the time came that he had to be put to sleep, Jack said that the hardest thing they ever had to do was to hold Wolf on the table while the doctor gave him the injection. All these years later the memory still brings tears to his eyes.

Jack has written on more than one occasion about his ongoing battle with depression, anxiety attacks and his recurring dreams and nightmares. The plot in his dreams has been the same every night for years, but the characters and scenery are different each time. The constants are; that he is in a strange place, he's trying to solve problems that confront him, and he is trying to find his way to where he belongs. He wonders if any of this might be connected to their years of traveling, always on the road, of being in strange places and never having a constant home.

Sometimes in these dreams he's trying to get to his hotel room, or the place where their show is supposed to be, but most often he's trying to get home. He can be walking down streets, searching for something, but when he turns around to go back the streets are different, as though he's made a wrong turn somewhere, often ending up in a dangerous neighborhood. In his dreams he is often trying to phone 'home' and occasionally a member of his immediate family answers. He forgets, until he wakes up, that they have all passed away long ago. Near the end of one dream, a woman took his arm and asked, "Are you all right?" He answered her, saying, "I think I may have Alzheimer's. I don't know where I am". He often wonders what, or where, 'home' really is, but he says writing about his dreams helps, and is much cheaper than therapy. Another way he copes with his depression and fears is by using humor and wisecracks. He worked as a stand-up comedian for a while in the early days.

He has also shared about his frustrations with the music industry and the lack of taste amongst so many listeners of country music, with their inability to discern good music from bad. In regard to the ongoing argument about what real country music is, he says, "If it sounds country, it is country". Jack believes music should be listened to and enjoyed, rather than argued about. He and Misty enjoy a wide variety of music, which includes traditional country, especially indie country as there is so much choice there. However they enjoy almost any kind of music, so long as it it good – including some classical music. They particularly enjoy music by Harry Nilsson, Harlan Howard, Roger Miller, The Beatles, Irving Berlin, the Gershwins, Randy Newman, Mickey Newbery, Tom T. Hall, Hoagy Carmichael, Van Morrison, Bonnie Raitt, Donald Fagen, Oscar Peterson, Willie Nelson, Credence Clearwater Revival and Gene Autry, amongst others.

Over the years Jack has studied a variety of religions and philosophies and has read several translations of the Christian Bible.

He has described how he has passed through various stages of religious zeal, agnosticism and atheism, and how he has wrestled with this huge concept all his life. He says that atheism is the easiest position to argue from, as it puts the burden onto the believer to prove the unprovable. He is still unsure where he stands on the matter. In spite of the fact that he was brought up as a Protestant and Misty as a Catholic, this has never been an issue between them.

He hates to discuss his beliefs, particularly with those he feels are preaching at him. He also hates political arguments, with a strong aversion to people who bad-mouth those who don't agree with their own political viewpoint. However he is happy for people to know that, when it comes to voting, both he and Misty are Democrats.

Human nature, with all its quirks and interactions, is another thing he has studied: love and friendship; strife and war; disagreements, prejudice and hate; and many other facets of life as he sees it. These studies have given him fuel for his songwriting, furnishing him with many of the subjects and situations he's needed to bring his lyrics to life.

Both he and Misty hate flying, though Jack says it is less about the flying, more about the fear of possibly crashing. They flew a lot during the seventies, due to their hectic schedule, but they both drank alcohol back then and they never flew completely sober. Pre-stage fright is another thing he has always suffered from but, once on stage, his nerves vanish. Whenever he could, he would get someone to play chess with him while he waited for his name to be called. He didn't care if he won or lost, just so long as it took his mind off the wait and calmed his nerves.

His inbuilt stubborn streak, wanting to do things his own way, and his resistance to accepting the advice of others, showed in his reluctance to play the cover songs that some of their audiences often wanted. By his own admission, he did not like singing covers and he would far rather sing only his own and Misty's songs, even though this has lost them bookings at times.

He says that he will never "act his age" or "grow old gracefully", nor will he cut off his shoulder-length hair. He has also said that he intends to lie about his age at every opportunity and that he plans to get a face-lift on his 90th birthday, though he is unlikely to need this as he is fortunate enough to have retained his very youthful looks. He zealously guards his and Misty's public image, convinced that this is necessary in order that people will listen to their music and take them seriously. He remains unconvinced that their fans are able to appreciate that their music is good enough for them to want to hear it on its own merit.

Their early hits were a double edged sword in that, while they got the attention that they were after, the novelty of those early hit songs, and the way Jack and Misty dressed, made it hard for them to be accepted by the Nashville community as serious singers of country music. He has composed many good country songs which were, and still are, good enough to be hits. They have, however, had some recent success, with several of their songs charting on the on-line indie charts. However the business and marketing side of the music industry has never been Jack's strong point and, though many of their songs are potential hits, he has never succeeded in getting any other artists, who might have been able to take their songs to the top of the charts, to cover any of them.

He loves to make people laugh and he is not beyond springing a practical joke now and then. There was the time when they were working in Key West during the sixties when their lead guitarist, Doug Tarrant, found a huge dead fish on the back seat of his new car. So what did they do? They wrapped the fish in a blanket and put it in an alley by the Downtowner. They then called the police to report finding a dead body. The police arrived, sirens wailing, and

Jack and his friends watched from their hiding place as the officers searched the alley. When they found the fish, they self-consciously looked round to see if anyone was watching, before driving off again. Nowadays his jokes are less practical and more verbal, particularly on Facebook, where he has regular followers awaiting the next one.

Jack spends a lot of time on the computer, either remastering music or trying to maintain a good on-line presence. Misty, by contrast, is a workaholic – always finding something to do. She is the one who ensures that day-to-day tasks get done, who takes care of the routine maintenance of their car, who runs round doing the shopping, collecting their mail from the Post Office, going to the bank and the laundromat, cooking, cleaning and scrubbing – inside and out – and looking after the gardening.

Meanwhile Jack once said that he would prefer to not move any muscles, apart from his breathing muscles. As he put it, "Laziness has been my inspiration. I became a musician to keep from getting a job. I do some of my best work while sitting still and staring out a window. I do a minimum of exercise to stay alive, but I don't like it very much. I brag about it after I do it".

Both Jack and Misty hate lightning and thunderstorms. They have had a couple of close calls with lightning, like the time when Jack had the phone knocked out of his hand by it. They are always relieved when the storm is over.

Watching a bit of television or playing their keyboards, either together or solo, provides evening relaxation. Then at the end of the day, after many a long hour at the computer, Jack likes to retire to bed with an audio book. Some of his favorite authors are Mark Twain, Dean Koontz, Elmore Leonard, J.R.R. Tolkien, Robert B. Parker, William Kottswinkle, Peter Straub, Douglas Adams and Stephen King. He enjoys books with suspense, mystery, humor and excitement to the story or "a trip through the light fantastic". His favorite book narrator is Frank Muller. Sadly Frank was unable to record any more books after he sustained serious brain damage in a motorcycle accident in 2001. He died in 2008.

Looking back, Jack said that two of his biggest thrills during his career were, first, when Roger Miller told him he was a fan of theirs before Jack got a chance to tell him he was also a fan of Roger. The second was on the street in Nashville, when the great songwriter, Harlan Howard, told Jack that he was his favorite songwriter. Compliments indeed.

CHAPTER 11

The Rewards of Success

Jack has been a prolific songwriter since the sixties. Though he wrote a few songs before then, these were not country music songs. However, after turning to country music, success came quickly. After changing their style in 1967, they got their big break with 'Tennessee Birdwalk', for which they won both the Billboard Country Music Award for Duo of the Year and a Grammy Nomination in the category for Best Country Music Vocal Performance – Duo or Group. Fourteen more of their songs made it into the charts during the next few years.

Jack has the ability to 'paint with words'. The lyrics he has written evoke a clear picture of the scenery and characters depicted. This is true both of his wacky novelty songs and of his serious songs. Words like "Carolina sundown red, making the mountains gingerbread", "Home – a place in my mind with summertime snow, Home – a place in my mind where wintertime flowers grow" and "Our Room: No masquerade, no costumes; Just aftershave and perfume, In Our Room" all vividly set the scene for the songs. There are numerous other similar examples from other songs, the lyrics for which can be found on their website. This line from their biggest hit is another image that sticks in the mind, "Take away their feathers and the birds will walk around in underwear".

Of the one hundred and nine songs listed, only seventeen of them have not been written, or co-written, by Jack. He found it hard to write songs under pressure, but with recording sessions every couple of months during the seventies, they were always facing a dead-line to come up with four or five new songs, which were not only good, but were different enough to attract the attention of the public. If Jack couldn't write enough songs, the recording company would have picked songs for them, a situation they wished to avoid if possible.

As already seen earlier in this book, Jack and Misty shared stages with almost all the big names of that era. They have also appeared on numerous television shows all round the USA, including such places as Alaska, San Francisco, Los Angeles, Philadelphia, Key West, the Kennedy Center and Washington D.C. These included appearances on the Dick Clark American Bandstand and The Robert W. Morgan Show. They also had a number of appearances on the Ralph Emery Show. Jack said that Ralph hated to interview him because he would answer his questions with a wisecrack, instead of a serious answer. Instead Ralph would turn to Misty for the serious answer he wanted.

They have received many favorable reviews of their music, a few of which are quoted below.

From a letter from Alex Cullum (DJ at Boots 'n' Saddle Radio, Norway)

"I am constantly overwhelmed by the 'niceness' of country folk. People I have never met and most probably (with my life expectancy) never will … write to me as though I am a member of their family… and I am just an ordinary person . So I can understand why people want to mark their affection for Misty and yourself. You are artists… you bring joy to thousands of People. Your words … words that you have written … give a happiness to your fans that cannot be obtained in any other way.

"Maybe some of them are like myself ...handicapped ... and find some things difficult to do, but we can listen. Who in their right mind could not be moved by 'Just one more song'. Who could refuse that inward smile when confronted with 'Tennessee Bird Walk'. For many of us ... you both, are the light at the end of the tunnel. You both help us to face, what sometimes is a difficult day. So just keep on, keeping on. If all else fails in life ...your fans know that 'Jack and Misty' are there, maybe not for ever... but your songs and music will be ... Thank you to you both for being exactly who you are ... 'Jack and Misty' ... Hilsen Alex."

★ ★ ★ ★ ★

Three reviews by Dan Michel
DJ and Program Director WPMB and WKRV-FM, Vandalia, Illinois

"Jack Blanchard and Misty Morgan take a classic situation... good love, gone bad and give it their trademark treatment...Jack and Misty capture the melancholy feeling in the lyrics with their deliberate but delicate vocals...The vocals float on a beautiful music arrangement that doesn't get in the way of the feeling the song is trying to sell...This one would sound great coming out of the speakers of a car radio...driving down a lonely stretch of highway... RINGS OF GOLD is a mellow mid-tempo winner from Jack Blanchard and Misty Morgan."

"You swear you've heard that song before...But you don't know when or where. Was it in a movie?...Was it in a Broadway musical?... It's instant familiarity the first time you hear it. One thing you'll know for sure when you hear "Blues Come In From The Rain" is that it's Jack Blanchard and Misty Morgan doing the singing ...... I don't know when Jack Blanchard wrote this song, but it has a kind of timeless quality about it…brilliant lyrics…a sweet melody… and an easy mid-tempo pace that'll make you want to sing along. It's the classic tale of a love gone wrong and the regrets that follow… A theme that has been used again and again in country and pop music… But it's so much more well done when it's written by a master songwriter, and performed by a duo that put it all on the line when they record a song …… I've listened to it three more times as I've written these words… But it's more fun if you listen for yourself… Check out Jack Blanchard and Misty Morgan's "Blues Come In From The Rain"… I think it'll be easy to hear that this song is a winner."

"I love this one! … "Just One More Song" by Jack Blanchard and Misty Morgan is built on a classic country arrangement…That enhances…but does not get in the way of the vocals… The song explores a classic country music theme…It's a break up song!…But it's a break up song that describes a graceful exit…Two lovers that appreciate each other and will look back fondly on the good memories that they made…Both Jack and Misty are in great voice… Showing more depth than they did in younger years…Jack effortlessly hits some dramatically low notes…And Misty's voice has gained a more soulful and bluesy tone over the years…But the highlight is when they harmonize…The harmonies captured here are among the best they have put on record …… a timeless classic country sound…It will sound great coming out of radio speakers as well as home stereo speakers on a hot summer day or a steamy summer night…It's a winning song…Made stronger by a winning performance by Jack and Misty."

Dan

★ ★ ★ ★ ★

July 7-8, 2007 The WEEKEND AUSTRALIAN COUNTRY
Sean Rabin's review of 'Weird Scenes Inside the Birdhouse', Jack Blanchard and Misty Morgan, Omni/Fuse

"Few words can prepare a listener for the music of married duo Jack Blanchard and Misty Morgan. "Lysergic Hayseed Melancholy and Cowpoke Philosophy" boasts a sticker on the front of the CD, but that's just part of it. After scoring a big hit in 1970 with Tennessee Bird Walk, Jack and Misty struggled to repeat their success. The songs on this compilation date from 1973 to 1976, when the Florida duo knew the charts were behind them but music wasn't. While songs such as Cows and The Cockroach Stomp continue their novelty vein, experience has undoubtedly taught them how quickly a joke grows tired, so along with the black humour and wry wordplay comes some fantastically catchy electric country music. With lush string accompaniment, smooth keyboards and gospel harmonies, Jack and Misty reveal themselves to be genre-benders, effortlessly marrying doo-wop with square dance or slide guitar with disco. Eccentric and accomplished, entertaining and subversive, this is a delicious '70s time capsule, confirming that no one has sounded quite like Jack and Misty."

★ ★ ★ ★ ★

April 2006 – Review by Pete Smith (Country Music Journalist & Broadcaster in the UK) of Jack and Misty's album 'Life and Death (And Almost Everything Else') (Omni)

"Jack Blanchard and Misty Morgan were both born in Buffalo, New York, and though both were childhood prodigies on the keyboards they did not meet until several years later and several hundred miles from New York. Jack and Misty were working in separate clubs almost next door to each other in Florida. By this time Jack had added slide guitar, lap steel, Dobro, and synthesisers to his instrumental skills whilst Misty stayed mainly with keyboards and vocals. Jack had also recorded a couple of solo singles, without success, before meeting and marrying Misty. After Blanchard's band dissolved the couple went out as a duo and in 1970 hit the number one spot with the novelty number "Tennessee Birdwalk", written by Jack. This was followed by another novelty Blanchard composition "Humphrey The Camel" and a country version of the Roger Cook / Roger Greenaway song "You've Got Your Troubles (I've Got Mine)" during that same year. The duo continued to enjoy minor hits until the mid-seventies, but that earlier success was now firmly in the past. Jack wrote humorous articles and drew comic strips for various newspapers, whilst he and Misty continued writing songs for themselves and other artists.

"Jack and Misty's marriage has survived longer than most in the music business, as has their popularity. The duo has remained extremely popular on the independent scene, where their records are regularly featured in a number of top tens. It is a crying shame that Jack and Misty did not repeat the success of 1970, for, as the newly released compilation, "Life and Death (And Almost Everything Else" (Omni), shows, the duo has recorded many sides equal or superior to that trio of major hits.

"The album's 29 tracks cover the period 1967-1973, a period some might describe as the duo's golden days, though I would disagree, for I see the last decade as probably Jack and Misty's most creative. However, this album presents a unique chance to sample six years in the life of a devoted and talented couple. Those three hits are included here plus 26 other great songs including "Chapel Hill", "Bethlehem Steel", "The Clock Of St. James", "Somewhere In Virginia In The Rain" (a particular favourite of mine), and "A Handful Of Dimes". There is plenty of humour too with "Yellow Bellied Sapsucker", "How I Lost 31 Pounds In 17 Days", and "If Eggs Had Legs". Wonderful stuff!"

www.worldwentdown.com/omni

The Rewards of Success

★ ★ ★ ★ ★

Three Reviews by Ray Grundy (www.metrocountry.co.uk)

Of 'Back From The Dead – Volume 2'

" … Since the mid 70s Jack & Misty had seemingly, disappeared from the Country Music scene, but now they make a very welcome return with the 23 track "Back From The Dead 2," a compilation of their hits and more all on one CD. Jack has a wonderful and very distinctive (a rarity in country music these days) deep, croaky voice that is complimented (sic) very well by Misty, producing superb harmonies of the sort you just can't get enough of. This compilation of both the straight and quirky side of the couple is a must have in any serious country music fans collection. If you already have their music on vinyl, then seize the chance to replace them on CD."

Of 'A Little Out Of Sync'

" … Of the 19 (tracks), 18 are originals while the other is an excellent version of the Patsy Cline hit, "Heartache." From catchy love songs like, "Because We Love," "A Handful Of Dimes" and the slow ballad, "Safe Harbor," through humerous songs like, "Starvin' Hog Blues," "Humphrey The Camel," "Fire Hydrant #79" and the Dixie flavoured, "I'm Washing Harry Down The Sink" to the story of a failed country band in "Rusty & The Cowboys," and the closing "Motel Time," a sing-a-long, barroom type song, the album is an absolute joy to listen to! Their superb harmonies are spellbinding! Latest single to be taken from the album is, "Here Today, Gone Tomorrow," a very catchy, Gospel flavoured song, that is sure to do well in the charts for them … Jack & Misty are certainly one of my favourite duo's around. I absolutely love Jack's deep baritone voice, which is complemented well by Misty's superb harmonies. I have no hesitation whatsoever in making this excellent album one of Metro Country's "Album's Of The Month" for January 2002.

Of 'Life and Death (And Almost Everything Else)'

" … They moved to Mega in 1971 and scored such hits as "There Must Be More to Life (Than Growing Old)" and "The Legendary Chicken Fairy," then in 1973, the two moved to Epic and had their last major hit, "Just One More Song." The duo have since enjoyed success on the Indie World Country charts as singles off their self-released "Back From the Dead" albums hit number one … Now, Australian record company 'The Omni Recording Corporation', have jumped in and put their money behind the duo, to release this bumper collection of their past recordings. And a big hand goes out to them for doing so!!"

★ ★ ★ ★ ★

Awards Received:

1970 – Grammy Nomination for Best Duo or Group of the Year
In 1971 Jack and Misty attended the 13th Annual Grammy Awards which were held in California. They had been nominated for the award for the Best Duo or Group (1970). The other contenders for this award were The Statler Brothers, Porter Wagoner & Dolly Parton, Johnny Cash & June Carter and Waylon Jennings & Jessi Colter. The winners were Johnny Cash & June Carter singing 'If I Were a Carpenter'. This was the first time that the CMA Awards show was televised.

1970 – Gold Record for Nations #1 Record – 'Tennessee Birdwalk' (March 1970)

1970 – CMA Citation of Merit Award as a FINALIST in the 1970 Annual Country Music Awards for Vocal Group of The Year (14th October 1970)

1970 – Billboard 1970 Country Music Award for Best Duo, Singles (presented 6th March 1971)

1970 – BMI (Broadcast Music, Inc.) Citation of Achievement (1970) in recognition of popularity in the country music field as measured by broadcast performances attained by 'Tennessee Birdwalk'.

1970 – 4th April: Appearance on the Grand Ole Opry along with Jack Green, Jeanie Seeley, Wilma Lee and Stony Cooper, Ernie Ashworth, Leroy Van Dyke, Ernest Tubb, Grandpa Jones, Bill Anderson, Marty Robbins, Archie Campbell, Stringbean, Jim & Jessie, Stu Phillips, Snuffy Miller and others.

1971 – BMI (Broadcast Music, Inc.) Citation of Achievement (1971) in recognition of popularity in the country music field as measured by broadcast performances attained by 'Humphrey the Camel'.

1970 – ASCAP Award for 'You've Got Your Troubles'.

2004 – Induction into the New York Country Music Hall of Fame

2010 – Induction into the Buffalo (NY) Music Hall of Fame

Their Singles★ (see page 119):

1956 – As The Dawn Breakers (Buddy Baker, Jim Warne, Don Fronczak, and Jackie Blanchard)
Boy With the Be-Bop Glasses / The Things I Love [Coral 61619]

1965 – As Jackie Blanchard & The Rockin' Impallas:
The King O'Hearts / Only A Fool [MIDA 111]

1965 – As Maryanne Mail (Misty) with Paul Gale (Tenor Sax):
The Tonga Torch / Let's Have A Hayride [Zodiac 3340]

1965 – As The Jack Blanchard Group with the Doug Wayne Guitars:
Gemini / New World [Zodiac 3341]
(NOTE: The Ventures covered 'Gemini' [Dolton #311] which effectively killed the Jack Blanchard version.)

1965 – As Jacqueline Hyde (Misty):
Strange New World / Runaway [Zodiac (number unknown)]

1965 – As Maryanne Mail (Misty) with Rusty Diamond:
Lonely Sentry / I Guess I'd Better Get Up And Go Home [Starday 747]
(NOTE: According to Jack, this A side also appeared on the Starday LP 'Country Music Goes To War'.)

As Jack Blanchard & Misty Morgan

1967/8 – Bethlehem Steel / No Sign Of Love
Those DARN Records 2041(a)/2042 (b) [Reissued on Wayside 1024 in 1969]

1969 – Big Black Bird (The Spirit Of Our Love) / The Autumn Song (On A Yellow Day)
Wayside 1028 [#59] [Reissued as Wayside/Smash WS-45-000]

1969 – Changin' Times / Poor Jody
Wayside/Smash WS-45-007

1970 – Tennessee Bird Walk / The Clock Of St. James
Wayside/Smash WS-45-010 [#1 country (2 wks)] [#23 pop]

1970 – Humphrey The Camel / A Place In My Mind
Wayside/Smash WS-45-013 [#5 country] [#78 pop]

1970 – You've Got Your Troubles (I've Got Mine) / How I Lost 31 Pounds In 17 Days
Wayside/Smash WS-45-015 [#27]

1971 – There Must Be More To Life (Than Growing Old) [#25]/ Fire Hydrant #79 [#46]
Mega 615-0031 (Their only double-sided hit)

1971 – Somewhere In Virginia In The Rain / If Eggs Had Legs
Mega 615-0046 [#15]

1972 – The Legendary Chicken Fairy / The Night We Heard The Voice
Mega 615-0063 [#38]

1972 – Washin' Harry Down The Sink / Miami Sidewalks
Mega 615-0082

1972 – Second Tuesday In December /Don't It Make You Want To Go Home
Mega 615-0089 [#60]

1973 – A Handful Of Dimes / It Seems Like There Ain't No Going Home
Mega 615-0101 [#65]

1973 – Shadows Of The Leaves / Sweet Memories
Mega 615-0114

1973 – The Cockroach Stomp / Carolina Sundown Red
Epic 5-11030

1973 – Just One More Song / Why Did I Sleep So Long?
Epic 5-11058 [#23]

1974 – Something On Your Mind / Here Today & Gone Tomorrow
Epic 5-11097 [#53]

1974 – Down To The End Of The Wine / You Can't Say I Didn't Try
Epic 8-50023 [#41]

1975 – The House (That Used To Be A Home)/ Cows
Epic 8-50082

1975 – Because We Love / It's Me (a.k.a "Starvin' Hog Blues")
Epic 8-50122 [#74]

1975 – I'm High On You / Let's Pretend
Epic 8-50181 [#68]

1975 – We've Still Got Each Other
Unknown – later released on Velvet Saw

1976 – Motel Time / Forty-Seven Miles
Epic 8-50205

1976 – Molasses In The Moonlight / Hands
Epic 8-50245

1977 – Living Together / Tennessee Bird Walk (remake)
United Artists UA-XW1004

1977 – Heartaches / You Come So Easy To Me
United Artists UA-XW1067

1979 – Tennessee Bird Walk / unknown
King GT4-2092

1979 – Somewhere In Virginia In The Rain / Cotton Blossom
Autumn Hill AH 1015+

1980 – Safe Harbor / I Will
Nu-Sound (number unknown)

1980 – Asleep In The Saddle / Island Of Love
Nu-Sound 80N-440/441

According to Jack, they also recorded one or two more 45s on the Autumn Hill label during the 80s. This small label was owned by an old friend from Miami, Jim Voytek. Jack believes the other recordings were 'Asleep In the Saddle' and possibly 'Try'. However Jim had an unexpected heart attack and died before they could get the records going.

After Jack entered the computer age he started to send songs to DJs at internet radio stations, and their songs began to get airplay on various indie labels, reaching a new audience.

2000 – Somewhere In Virginia In The Rain
Song 1 (number unknown) #5 (IndieWorld chart)

2000 – Rings Of Gold
Song 1 (number unknown) #1 (IndieWorld chart)

2001 – Just One More Song
Stardust International

2001 – Shadows Of The Leaves
Stardust International #29 (May 2001)

2001 – Call On Me
Stardust International #30 (June 2001)

2002 – Rusty and The Cowboys
WHP Records (Feb. 2002)

2002 – There Must Be More To Life (Than Growing Old)
Song 1 #4 (March 2002 – Indieworld chart)

2002 – Seems Like There Ain't No Goin' Home
Stardust International #35 (March 2002)

2002 – Fire Hydrant #79
Stardust International #37 (May 2002)

2002 – Somewhere In Virginia In The Rain
Stardust International #38 (July 2002)

2003 – Sweet Memories
Stardust International #41 (February 2003)

2003 – Safe Harbor
Stardust International #42 (April 2003)

2003 – Perry Mason Rides Again (instrumental)
Roto Noto Records [Canada] (June 23, 2003)

2003 – Bethlehem Steel
Stardust International #43 (June 2003)

2003 – Washing Harry Down The Sink
Stardust International #44 (August 2003)

2003 – You Come So Easy To Me
Stardust International #45 (October 2003)

2004 – The House (That Used To Be A Home)
Stardust International #48 (March 2004)

2004 – Carolina Sundown Red
Stardust International #49 (May 2004)

2004 – Shadow Of A Big Black Bird
Stardust International #50 (July 2004)

2004 – If Eggs Had Legs
Stardust International #51 (Sept. 2004)

2005 – Try / Still Comin' Down
Stardust International #53 (April 2005)

2005 – High On You
Stardust International #54 (June 2005)

2005 – I Will
Stardust International #56 (November 2005)

2006 – The Sunset Train
Stardust International #60 (January 2006)

2006 – The Voice
Stardust International #61 (March 2006)

2006 – Rings Of Gold
Stardust International #62 (July 2006)

2006 – Motel Time
Stardust International #63 (September 2006)

2006 – 47 Miles (to the Georgia line)
Stardust International #64 (November 2006)

2007 – When Blues Come In From The Rain
Stardust International #65 (January 2007)

They have had other charted songs since this date on various indie charts, but no details have been recorded

Their CDs★ (see page 119):

1992 – 'Back In Harmony'
Playback PCD 4512 (CD) Produced by Jack Gale.

1999 – 'Back From The Dead, Volume 2', their debut self-produced CD
Velvet Saw 1201.

2001 – Jack & Misty's second Velvet Saw CD, 'A Little Out Of Sync'
Velvet Saw 0801 (August)

2001 – 'Masters Of The Keyboards'
Jack and Misty's first ever instrumental album
Velvet Saw VS 0901 (September)

2001 – 'Jack and Misty Are CRAZY!'
Velvet Saw 1101 (November)

2004 – 'Beginnings'
Velvet Saw VS 1104 (December)

2006 – 'Two Sides… One More Time!'
Archeological Records AR 0806 (August)
A re-issue of their long-out-of-print 1972 Mega album

2008 – 'Life And Death (and almost everything else.)'
OMNI-102 Australian import

2008 – 'Weird Scenes Inside The Birdhouse'
OMNI-107 Australian import (2008)

2008 – 'Nashville Sputnik': Various artists singing the songs of Jack Blanchard and Misty Morgan. OMNI-115 Australian import (2009)

2009 – 'Traveling Music'
VS 10059 (August) www.cdbaby.com/cd/jackmisty

★ Thanks go to Jack Blanchard, The Record Finder, recordmaster.com and Ken Pobo for helping Jerry compile this discography by supplying valuable discographical info (especially on some of the more obscure titles). All the chart positions are as they appeared in Billboard Magazine's country [and pop] charts copyright ©1969-1975 BPI Communications, Inc. (Reproduced by permission of Jerry Withers)

CHAPTER 12

The Last Word ... from Jack

"We have made a bunch of beautiful recordings that can never be country singles because they don't fit the narrow "Old Country" or "New Country" molds.
Some may have a couple of chords too many,
or maybe some strings in the background.
But they are fine chord changes that fit the songs, and the strings were recorded in an era when there was more freedom.

"The studio musicians tell us they really like doing our music. They are so used to holding back to fit into the two main country markets, that it's refreshing for them to stretch their musical wings.

"We'll keep on doing our thing, even if we don't get rich at it. We don't fit into any of the pigeonholes.
Some of our music is traditional and some is not,
but it's honest, and not decided by what is commercial."

Jack Blanchard and Misty Morgan

And finally, as Misty always likes to have the very last word, I am adding a quote from her taken from their interview with the late Mark Harris which was mentioned on page 68.

She says, "I believe that music is an art and should be carried on its own merit. Nobody cares how Rembrandt or Picasso looked. Their art speaks for itself." Misty continues, "I really don't like the way they are selling sex instead of the music today. It suggests something may be lacking in the music."

Acknowledgements

My heartfelt thanks go to the following for their contributions towards the information needed for this biography and for all the help and support I have been given:

Jack Blanchard and Misty Morgan: for Jack's columns and stories, plus all the e-mails from them and the many hours spent talking together, both face-to-face and by phone.

Their friends and family members: for adding facts and filling in details from their recollections.

Jerry Withers: for the background facts about the setting up of Jack and Misty's website (http://www.jackandmisty.com) and for his permission for my use of his discography of their music.

Peter Berlin: about how he met them, his contribution in helping Jerry set up the website and his help as Jack was learning how to use a computer.

Gayle Noble: about how she got to know them, her help in solving Jack's computer problems and her role in the design of several of their promotional images. Also many thanks to her for the use of the striking compilation photograph used in the design of the book cover.

Marli Slater: about her role in helping them become better known on the internet through her website, My Kind of Music (http://www.mkoc.com).

Wikipedia and the Internet: for checking general facts, name origins and information about places mentioned.

Acknowledgements

All those whose reviews have provided quotes: Ray Grundy (http://www.metrocountry.co.uk); Dan Michel (DJ and Program Director WPMB and WKRV-FM, Vandalia, Illinois); Alex Cullum (DJ at Boots 'n' Saddle Radio, Norway); Pete Smith (Country Music Journalist & Broadcaster in the UK); Sean Rabin (The Weekend Australian Country).

Amazon.com: (http://www.amazon.com/Definitive-Country-Ultimate-Encyclopedia-Music/dp/0399521445) for giving me the correct title of the 1995 encyclopedia, 'Definitive Country: The Ultimate Encyclopedia of Country Music'. ISBN-10: 0399521445

A special thank you to Tom T. Hall, Ralph Emery, Jim Ed Brown, Lloyd Green, Steve Hall and Ron Oates for supplying the blurbs for the back cover.

And a HUGE thank you to Alice C. Bateman for doing an such excellent job of proofreading my manuscript and for supplying her blurb.

And last, but not least:

Matador Publishers: for all their help, advice and expertise in getting this book into print.

The Blurbs... In Full

"I am looking forward to reading the adventures of Jack and Misty. Wonderful friends who have made the world a better place with their music. If their biography is like their lives, which I'm sure it is, we're in for a helluva ride."
Tom T. Hall: The Storyteller / songwriter, Nashville, Tennessee.

"I have always enjoyed Jack and Misty's music. They visited my program many times during their career, and though I have not seen them in a long time, they are a Class 'A' couple."
Ralph Emery: Television host, Nashville, Tennessee.

"I recorded hundreds of records as steel guitarist and session leader for producer "Little" Richie Johnson on Wayside Records during the 1960s & 1970s. The only #1 hit to emerge from that smorgasbord of songs was Jack and Misty's "Tennessee Birdwalk", selling more than 1 ½ million records as #1 in the Billboard Country charts and as a sizeable hit in the pop charts. Bravo for those two intrepid singers!"
Lloyd Green: Renowned pedal steel guitarist, Nashville, Tennessee.

"I've always enjoyed (Jack & Misty's) singing, including 'Tennessee Birdwalk', and I'm glad they took the walk together."
Jim Ed Brown: Member of the Grand Ole Opry, Nashville, Tennessee.

IN HARMONY

"The hardest-working duo in show business. Jack and Misty have followed their passion for 4 ½ decades to the continued delight of their minions of fans. No matter your musical cup of tea, just sit in on a set of Jack's and Misty's... they are masters of it all. You'll be fans forever. Count on it."
Ron Oates: Jes Fine Productions, Nashville, Tennessee.

"I did a show years ago in Minnesota with Jack & Misty and I was just a kid so I got a real lesson on how to entertain a crowd. Not only were their songs cool but they had the crowd eating out of their hands with comedy... I know it has been 30 years but I still remember Jack telling the crowd that he doesn't touch anything in the bathroom... he flushes the toilet with his foot... he turns the water on and off with his elbows ... he said he doesn't even touch the door knob on the way out... he opens it with his teeth!"
Once I heard "Tennessee Bird Walk" I asked Jack how do you write a hit song? He said it was like making a horse out of clay.... he said you start with a big pile of clay and cut away everything that don't look like a horse! ...
I talked a lot with Jack because he wouldn't let me near Misty! I don't blame him!
Steve Hall / Shotgun Red: Nashville, Tennessee.

"Jack and Misty, so very much more than a Tennessee Bird Walk!"
Alice C. Bateman: Author, ONE AMERICAN DREAMER.

Contact Details

Jack's e-mail: jackandmisty@gmail.com
Website: http://www.jackandmisty.com
CD Baby: http://www.cdbaby.com/cd/jackmisty
SoundClick: http://www.soundclick.com (search for Jack/Misty)

Moragh's e-mail: MoraghC@gmail.com
Website: http://www.about.me/moraghcarter